Contents

GRADE **4**

W9-CTP-302

Review

Find the sums or differences.

① $\begin{array}{r} 627 \\ +\ 346 \\ \hline \end{array}$	② $\begin{array}{r} 545 \\ -\ 248 \\ \hline \end{array}$	③ $\begin{array}{r} 402 \\ +\ \ \ 87 \\ \hline \end{array}$	④ $\begin{array}{r} 913 \\ -\ \ \ 54 \\ \hline \end{array}$

⑤ $692 - 354 =$ _____   ⑥ $329 + 463 =$ _____

⑦ $291 + 482 =$ _____   ⑧ $842 - 786 =$ _____

⑨ $142 + 35 =$ _____   ⑩ $510 - 73 =$ _____

Fill in the missing numbers.

⑪ $4 +$ _____ $= 18$ ⑫ $33 -$ _____ $= 26$

⑬ $25 +$ _____ $= 32$ ⑭ _____ $+ 17 = 31$

⑮ _____ $- 9 = 29$ ⑯ _____ $+ 6 = 18$

Do the multiplication or division.

⑰ $\begin{array}{r} 8 \\ \times\ \ \ 9 \\ \hline \end{array}$	⑱ $\begin{array}{r} 6 \\ \times\ \ \ 7 \\ \hline \end{array}$	⑲ $\begin{array}{r} 4 \\ \times\ \ \ 5 \\ \hline \end{array}$	⑳ $\begin{array}{r} 9 \\ \times\ \ \ 3 \\ \hline \end{array}$
㉑ $3\overline{)12}$	㉒ $9\overline{)27}$	㉓ $7\overline{)35}$	㉔ $6\overline{)48}$
㉕ $8\overline{)26}$	㉖ $5\overline{)47}$	㉗ $9\overline{)46}$	㉘ $4\overline{)34}$

㉙ $2 \times 8 =$ _____   ㉚ $7 \times 5 =$ _____   ㉛ $3 \times 4 =$ _____

㉜ $40 \div 8 =$ _____   ㉝ $45 \div 6 =$ _____   ㉞ $32 \div 5 =$ _____

Choose the most appropriate unit to measure each of the following lengths. Write cm, m, or km.

㉟   The length of this book   _____

㊱   The width of your bedroom   _____

㊲   The distance from your home to your school   _____

㊳   The height of a giraffe   _____

㊴   The distance from Vancouver to Toronto   _____

Choose the most appropriate unit to measure each of the following masses. Write kg or g. Then put them in order from lightest to heaviest.

㊵

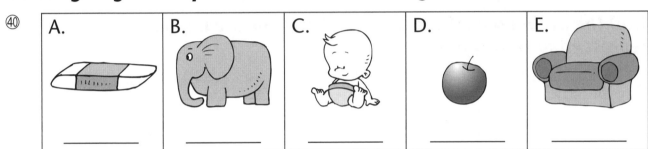

A.   _____   B.   _____   C.   _____   D.   _____   E.   _____

㊶   From lightest to heaviest : _____

Write the times to the nearest minutes.

㊷   _____   ㊸   _____   ㊹   _____

Write the number of lines of symmetry for each picture.

㊺   _____   ㊻   _____   ㊼   _____

Write a fraction for the shaded parts in each diagram.

48 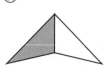 _____

49 _____

50 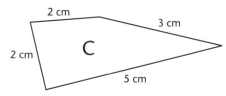 _____

51 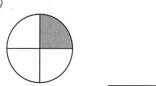 _____

52 _____

53 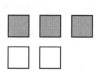 _____

Find the perimeters of the shapes. Then put them in order. Write their representing letters only.

54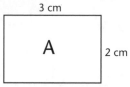

Shape	A	B	C
Perimeter			

55 From the one with greatest perimeter to the one with least :

_____

Look at the first picture. Then write 'reflection', 'rotation', or 'translation' to indicate how it is transformed.

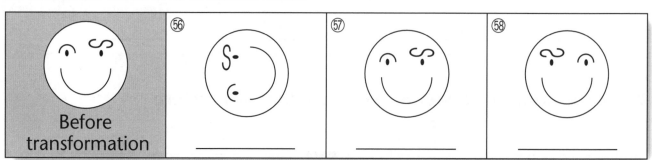

Before transformation

56 _____

57 _____

58 _____

Continue each pattern.

59 1 1 2 3 5 8 ____ ____

60  ____ ____

4

Name the solids and complete the table.

A 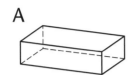   B   C   D

	Solid	Name	No. of faces	No. of edges	No. of vertices
⑥	A				
⑥	B				
⑥	C				
⑥	D				

This graph shows the favourite foods of the students in Ms. Smith's class. Read the graph and answer the questions.

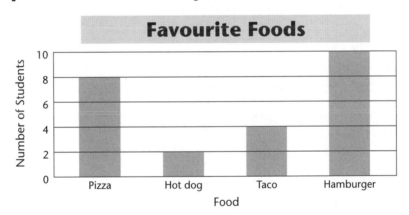

⑥⑤   Which food do most students like?   _____

⑥⑥   How many more students like hamburgers than hot dogs?   _____

⑥⑦   Which food is half as much as pizza?   _____

Answer the questions.

⑥⑧   Anna bought a bag of chips for 99¢ and a chocolate bar for $1.25. How much money did Anna spend? $ _____

⑥⑨   Michael had $5.25. He bought a magazine for $4.50. How much money does Michael have now? $ _____

⑦⓪   What are the total possible outcomes if you roll a dice?   _____

1 Numbers to 10 000

Write the number shown by each group of blocks in numerals.

Example

1 one

1 ten

1 hundred

1 thousand

In numerals : 2236

In words : Two thousand two hundred thirty-six

① _____

② _____

③ _____

Write the numbers in words.

④ 5239 _____

⑤ 7108 _____

⑥ 4620 _____

⑦ 3057 _____

Write the numerals.

⑧ Six thousand four hundred fifty-three _____

⑨ Nine thousand eighty-one _____

⑩ Eight thousand five hundred six _____

⑪ Five thousand seven hundred forty _____

Write the numbers.

Quick Tip

thousands
hundreds
tens
ones

6 2 3 5

6235
= 6 thousands 2 hundreds 3 tens 5 ones

⑫   5 thousands 7 hundreds 4 ones

　　_____

⑬   1 thousand 8 hundreds 2 tens 9 ones

　　_____

⑭   3 thousands 6 tens 5 ones　　　　　　　　　　　　_____

⑮   9 thousands 4 hundreds 2 tens　　　　　　　　　　_____

Fill in the correct digits.

⑯   2680 | | thousands | | hundreds | | tens | | ones |

⑰   7963 | | thousands | | hundreds | | tens | | ones |

⑱   4226 | | thousands | | hundreds | | tens | | ones |

Write the expanded form or standard form of each number.

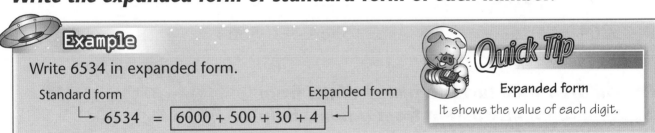

Example

Write 6534 in expanded form.

Standard form　　　　　　　　　　　Expanded form

　↳ 6534 = | 6000 + 500 + 30 + 4 | ↵

Quick Tip

Expanded form

It shows the value of each digit.

⑲   9586　　= 9000 + _____ + _____ + _____

⑳   2955　　= _____ + 900 + _____ + _____

㉑   8473　　= _____ + _____ + 70 + _____

㉒   _____　= 3000 + 200 + 60 + 7

㉓   _____　= 6000 + 30 + 8

㉔   _____　= 5000 + 700 + 40

Write the place value of each underlined digit.

㉕   8<u>3</u>26 _____　　　　㉖   49<u>1</u>0 _____

㉗   <u>5</u>741 _____　　　　㉘   604<u>9</u> _____

Aunt Anna sells candies and toys. Help her colour the candies or toys.

㉙ Colour the candies with the greatest numbers in stock.

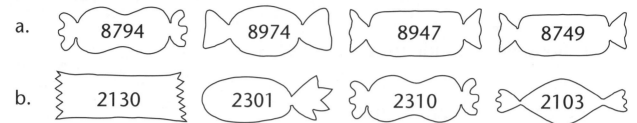

a. 8794 8974 8947 8749

b. 2130 2301 2310 2103

㉚ Colour the toys with the smallest numbers in stock.

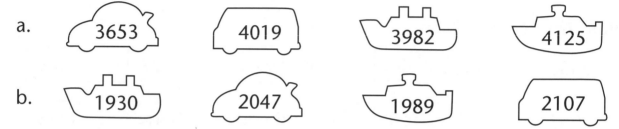

a. 3653 4019 3982 4125

b. 1930 2047 1989 2107

Fill in the missing numbers.

㉛ 6093 _____ 5893 5793 _____ _____

㉜ 2102 3102 _____ _____ 6102 _____

㉝ 5264 _____ _____ 5564 5664 _____

The children take turns to pick 4 digits from a bag, and an instruction from a box. Help the children form the 4-digit numbers following the instructions and answer the questions.

		Instruction	Digits picked	Number formed
㉞	Janice	The greatest possible number	2 , 3 , 0 , 1	
㉟	Pete	The smallest possible number	4 , 7 , 3 , 5	
㊱	Marie	The smallest odd number	3 , 8 , 1 , 6	
㊲	Tom	The greatest even number	5 , 9 , 4 , 2	

㊳ Who forms the greatest number? _____

㊴ Who forms the smallest number? _____

8

The counter of a photocopier records the number of copies made. Look at the counter readings of five photocopiers and answer the questions.

⑩ Which reading shows the most copies made? _____

㊶ Which reading shows the fewest copies made? _____

㊷ Which reading is seven hundred greater than 6143? _____

㊸ Which reading is four hundred smaller than 7863? _____

㊹ Which readings have 4 in the hundreds place? _____

㊺ Which readings have 7 in the thousands place? _____

㊻ Which two readings differ from 8536 by 1000? _____

㊼ Which two readings differ by 1 thousand 1 hundred? _____

㊽ Put the readings in order from smallest to greatest.

_____

MIND BOGGLER

What is the message?

Uncle Tim sent a message to Danny. Put the numbers in order from greatest to smallest, and write their representing letters. Then read the message.

E 7931   K 4386   T 5913   G 9317   R 4638   W 5319   A 7319   O 4678   R 9127

___ ___ ___ ___ ___   ___ ___ ___ ___ !

2 Addition and Subtraction

Do the addition. Follow the path of the sums greater than 7600 to help Janice find her toy.

Quick Tip

To do vertical addition, align all the numbers on the right. Add the ones first. Remember to add the digit carried over from the right.

①
```
  3 7 5 6
+ 4 2 8 3
```

②
```
  6 3 1 5
+ 3 4 9 7
```

③
```
  1 2 4 6
+ 2 3 9 1
```

④
```
  3 2 0 1
+ 1 4 6 8
```

⑤
```
  4 6 2 8
+ 1 9 1 9
```

⑥
```
  5 1 4 2
+   3 8 4
```

⑦
```
  1 9 8 5
+ 4 5 7 3
```

⑧
```
  2 0 8 6
+ 3 9 1 7
```

⑨ 9503 + 827 = _____

⑩ 2510 + 4695 = _____

⑪ 4028 + 3145 = _____

⑫ 1793 + 2118 = _____

⑬ 6537 + 924 = _____

⑭ 6872 + 2950 = _____

⑮ 4315 + 387 = _____

⑯ 7963 + 1048 = _____

⑰ 3196 + 4422 = _____

⑱ 8524 + 3191 = _____

⑲ 3217 + 5278 = _____

⑳ 6412 + 2412 = _____

㉑ 7216 + 913 = _____

㉒ 1361 + 2573 = _____

㉓ 2086 + 3967 = _____

㉔ 1496 + 5163 = _____

㉕

8039	8761	8824	8129
9812	7905	8495	7620
10 330	9822	11 715	9133
8213	9011	7618	8765

Do the subtraction.

㉖ $\begin{array}{r} 7321 \\ -\ \ 879 \\ \hline \end{array}$	㉗ $\begin{array}{r} 4821 \\ -\ \ 398 \\ \hline \end{array}$	
㉘ $\begin{array}{r} 9873 \\ -\ \ 538 \\ \hline \end{array}$	㉙ $\begin{array}{r} 6423 \\ -\ \ 946 \\ \hline \end{array}$	
㉚ $\begin{array}{r} 3271 \\ -\ \ 974 \\ \hline \end{array}$	㉛ $\begin{array}{r} 7408 \\ -\ \ 293 \\ \hline \end{array}$	㉜ $\begin{array}{r} 4620 \\ -\ \ 979 \\ \hline \end{array}$

Quick Tip

To do vertical subtraction, align all the numbers on the right. Subtract the ones first. If you can't take away, borrow 1 from the left.

㉝ 5206 – 378 = ____________ ㉞ 6087 – 558 = ____________

㉟ 2576 – 827 = ____________ ㊱ 4538 – 814 = ____________

㊲ 4398 – 673 = ____________ ㊳ 3879 – 609 = ____________

㊴ 9260 – 859 = ____________ ㊵ 5842 – 462 = ____________

Round the following numbers to the nearest hundred.

Example

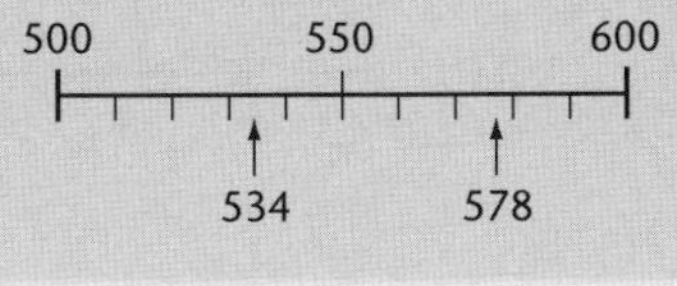
500
550
600
534
578

534 is closer to 500 while 578 is closer to 600, so 534 is rounded to 500 and 578 is rounded to 600. 550 is halfway between 500 and 600. It is rounded up to 600.

㊶ 294 → __________ ㊷ 315 → __________

㊸ 450 → __________ ㊹ 182 → __________

㊺ 537 → __________ ㊻ 128 → __________

Round the following numbers to the nearest thousand.

㊼ 7148 → __________ ㊽ 4803 → __________

㊾ 1963 → __________ ㊿ 6530 → __________

(51) 5298 → __________ (52) 8345 → __________

Estimate the sums or differences by rounding the 4-digit numbers to the nearest thousand and the 3-digit numbers to the nearest hundred. Then find the exact answers.

㊾ 7499 + 2501 = _____ **Estimate** _____ + _____ = _____

㊿ 6269 + 2721 = _____ **Estimate** _____ + _____ = _____

⑤ 6548 − 613 = _____ **Estimate** _____ − _____ = _____

㊻ 2138 + 1048 = _____ **Estimate** _____ + _____ = _____

㊼ 9236 − 703 = _____ **Estimate** _____ − _____ = _____

㊽ 5211 + 3650 = _____ **Estimate** _____ + _____ = _____

㊾ 7710 − 439 = _____ **Estimate** _____ − _____ = _____

㊿ 4721 + 1875 = _____ **Estimate** _____ + _____ = _____

㊱ 1030 − 250 = _____ **Estimate** _____ − _____ = _____

Answer the questions.

㊽ What number is 268 greater than 4735? _____

㊾ What is the number if 6739 is reduced by 215? _____

㊿ How much is the difference between $1650 and $450? _____

㊄ What is the digit in the tens place when you add 3829 and 2958? _____

㊅ What is the digit in the hundreds place when you subtract 978 from 2218? _____

㊇ What is the difference between the smallest 4-digit odd number and the greatest 3-digit number? _____

㊈ What is the sum of the greatest 3-digit even number and the smallest 4-digit odd number? _____

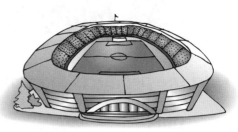

Solve the problems. Show your work.

⑥⑨ A football stadium has 970 seats in the red section, 1125 seats in the green section, and 2540 seats in the yellow section.

     a. How many seats are in the green and yellow sections altogether?

         _____ = _____

         _____ seats are in the green and yellow sections altogether.

     b. How many more seats are in the yellow section than the red section?

         _____ = _____

         _____ more seats are in the yellow section than the red section.

⑦⓪ Cameron helps out in the school library. The library has 3411 storybooks, 2936 picture books, and 424 French books.

     a. How many storybooks and picture books are there in the library?

         _____ = _____

     There are _____ storybooks and picture books in the library.

     b. How many more storybooks are there than French books?

         _____ = _____

     There are _____ more storybooks than French books.

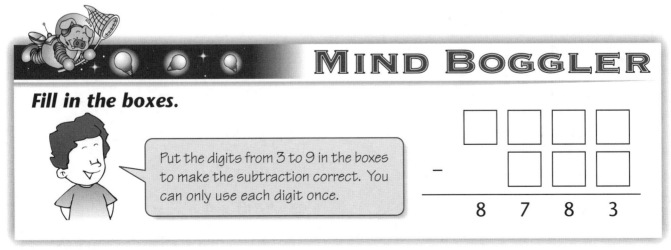

MIND BOGGLER

Fill in the boxes.

Put the digits from 3 to 9 in the boxes to make the subtraction correct. You can only use each digit once.

```
   □ □ □ □
 -   □ □ □
 ─────────
   8 7 8 3
```

3 Multiplication

Find the products mentally.

① 100 x 7 = _____

② 9 x 10 = _____

③ 8 x 1000 = _____

④ 10 x 5 = _____

⑤ 1000 x 2 = _____

⑥ 6 x 100 = _____

⑦ 3 x 1000 = _____

⑧ 12 x 100 = _____

⑨ 1000 x 15 = _____

Quick Tip

When you multiply a number by 10, just add 1 zero to the number. Add 2 zeros when you multiply it by 100, and 3 zeros when you multiply it by 1000.

Examples

① 2 x 20 = 2 x 2 x 10
= 4 x 10
= 40

② 300 x 4 = 100 x 3 x 4
= 100 x 12
= 1200

Find the products.

⑩ 3 x 80 = _____

⑪ 50 x 4 = _____

⑫ 4 x 600 = _____

⑬ 2 x 3000 = _____

⑭ 400 x 3 = _____

⑮ 2000 x 4 = _____

⑯ 400 x 7 = _____

⑰ 2 x 5000 = _____

⑱ 9 x 20 = _____

⑲ 5 x 400 = _____

⑳ 8 x 70 = _____

㉑ 90 x 5 = _____

㉒ 60 x 6 = _____

㉓ 700 x 9 = _____

㉔ 200 x 8 = _____

㉕ 4000 x 2 = _____

㉖ 500 x 6 = _____

㉗ 40 x 7 = _____

㉘ 3000 x 9 = _____

㉙ 900 x 4 = _____

Example

39 x 5 = ? `Long way`

```
      3 9    ← Align the numbers
  x     5       on the right.
      4 5    ← 5 x 9
    1 5 0    ← 5 x 30
    1 9 5    ← Add the products.
```

39 x 5 = 195

`Short way`

Multiply the ones first.

```
        4
      3 ⌐9⌐  ⌐ Align the
  x     ⌊5⌋    numbers on
        5 ←    the right.
```

5 x 9 = 45
Carry 4 tens to the tens.

Then multiply the tens.

```
        4
      ⌐3⌐ 9
  x      ⌊5⌋
    1 9 5
```

15 + 4 = 19
carried over from the ones

Multiply the long way.

③⁰
```
      1 6
  x     7
```

③¹
```
      4 3
  x     5
```

③²
```
      2 5
  x     8
```

③³
```
      5 2
  x     4
```

Multiply the short way.

③⁴
```
      7 2
  x     6
```

③⁵
```
      9 4
  x     5
```

③⁶
```
      2 8
  x     7
```

③⁷
```
      5 7
  x     8
```

③⁸
```
      4 6
  x     3
```

③⁹
```
      3 8
  x     4
```

⁴⁰
```
      6 8
  x     9
```

⁴¹
```
      9 2
  x     7
```

④² 28 x 9 = _____

④³ 36 x 9 = _____

④⁴ 76 x 8 = _____

④⁵ 43 x 5 = _____

④⁶ 53 x 6 = _____

④⁷ 81 x 7 = _____

④⁸ 25 x 3 = _____

④⁹ 4 x 68 = _____

⁵⁰ 5 x 62 = _____

⁵¹ 6 x 17 = _____

⁵² 3 x 72 = _____

⁵³ 8 x 53 = _____

⁵⁴ 9 x 34 = _____

⁵⁵ 7 x 46 = _____

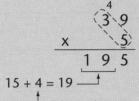

Quick Tip

Though the order of multiplication has changed, the product is still the same.
e.g. 4 x 68 = 68 x 4

Multiply the long way.

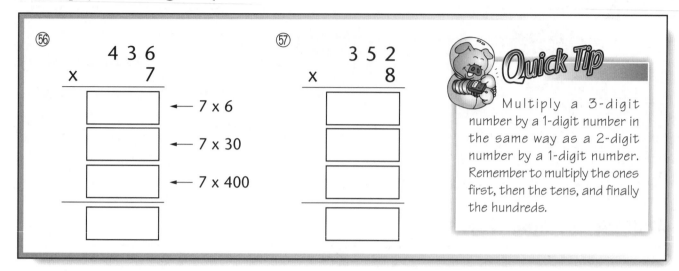

(56)

$$\begin{array}{r} 436 \\ \times \quad 7 \\ \hline \end{array}$$

☐ ← 7 x 6

☐ ← 7 x 30

☐ ← 7 x 400

☐

(57)

$$\begin{array}{r} 352 \\ \times \quad 8 \\ \hline \end{array}$$

☐

☐

☐

☐

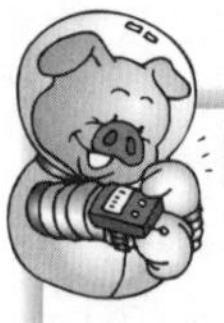

Quick Tip

Multiply a 3-digit number by a 1-digit number in the same way as a 2-digit number by a 1-digit number. Remember to multiply the ones first, then the tens, and finally the hundreds.

Multiply the short way.

(58) 296 x 7	(59) 478 x 5	(60) 639 x 9	(61) 764 x 3

(62) 847 x 2 = ______	(63) 729 x 4 = ______	(64) 352 x 9 = ______
(65) 4 x 526 = ______	(66) 925 x 6 = ______	(67) 8 x 648 = ______
(68) 7 x 388 = ______	(69) 509 x 2 = ______	(70) 5 x 183 = ______

Aunt Mary bought a lot of things. Help her find the total amount.

(71)

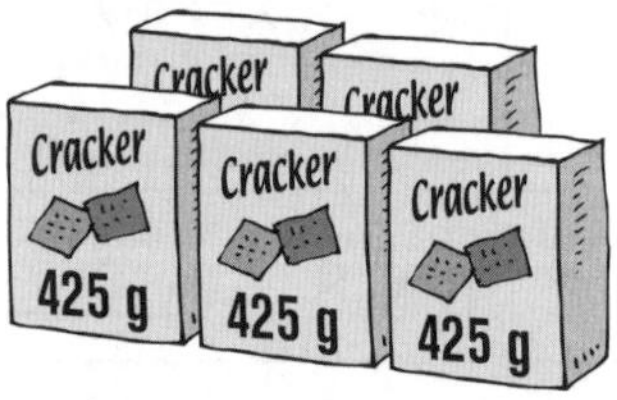

Total: ______ g

(72)

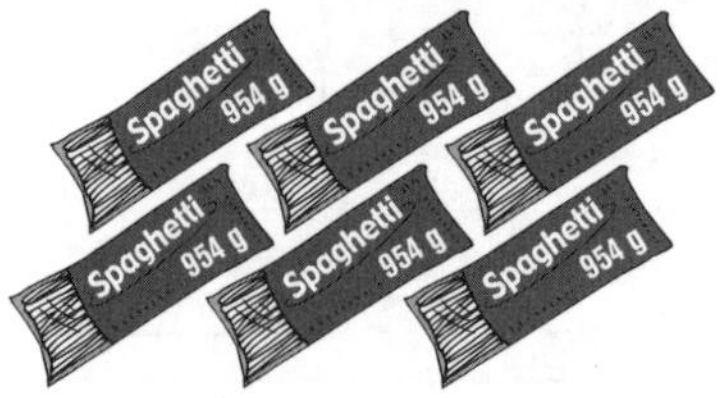

Total: ______ g

(73)

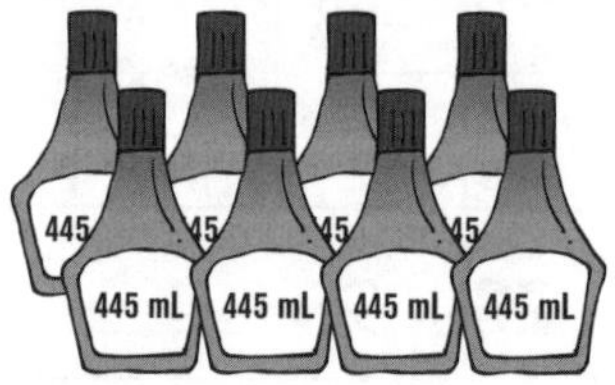

Total: ______ mL

(74)

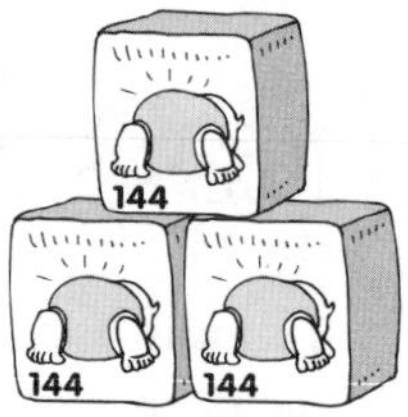

Total: ______ diapers

(75)

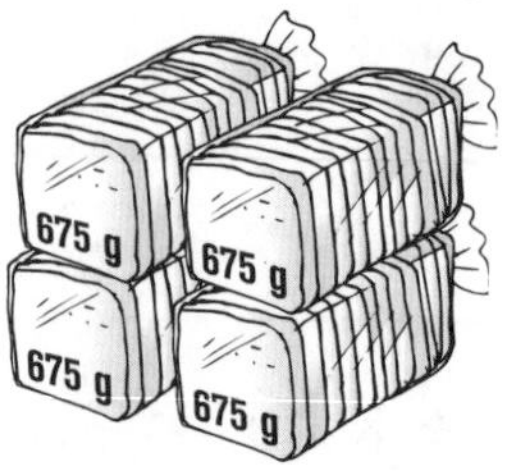

Total: ______ g

(76)

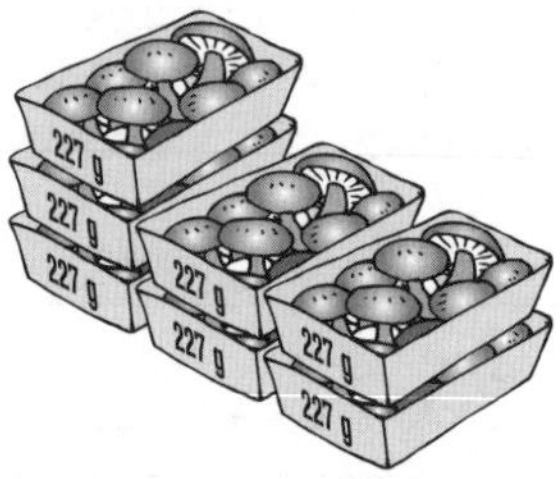

Total: ______ g

Solve the problems.

⑦⑦ Daniel and Michelle went apple-picking. They filled 7 baskets with 275 apples each. How many apples did they pick?

⑦⑧ Julian's school bus can carry 55 students each time. The bus is filled 6 times a day. How many students have been on the bus in one day?

⑦⑨ The bleachers of Julian's school have 5 sections. Each section can seat 125 people . How many people can sit in the bleachers?

⑧⓪ Amanda has 7 boxes of cookies for sale in a fundraising event. Each box contains 24 packages of cookies. How many packages of cookies will Amanda have to sell?

 **MIND BOGGLER**

What number am I?

> I'm a 2-digit number smaller than 50. When I'm multiplied by 7, the product is greater than 200. The sum of my digits is 5.

You are _____ .

4 Division I

Fill in the missing numbers.

① 80 ÷ 2 = _____ tens ÷ 2 = _____ tens = _____	② 900 ÷ 3 = _____ hundreds ÷ 3 = _____ hundreds = _____
③ 160 ÷ 4 = _____ tens ÷ 4 = _____ tens = _____	④ 450 ÷ 5 = _____ tens ÷ 5 = _____ tens = _____
⑤ 360 ÷ 6 = _____ tens ÷ 6 = _____ tens = _____	⑥ 700 ÷ 7 = _____ hundreds ÷ 7 = _____ hundred = _____

Do the division.

⑦ 160 ÷ 2 = _____   ⑧ 90 ÷ 3 = _____   ⑨ 50 ÷ 5 = _____

⑩ 80 ÷ 4 = _____   ⑪ 560 ÷ 8 = _____   ⑫ 900 ÷ 9 = _____

⑬ 630 ÷ 7 = _____   ⑭ 350 ÷ 5 = _____   ⑮ 180 ÷ 6 = _____

⑯ 140 ÷ 7 = _____   ⑰ 240 ÷ 8 = _____   ⑱ 450 ÷ 9 = _____

Round the dividends to the nearest ten. Then estimate the quotients.

⑲ 62 ÷ 3   Estimate ▶ _____ ÷ 3
 = _____

⑳ 78 ÷ 4   Estimate ▶ _____ ÷ 4
 = _____

㉑ 47 ÷ 5   Estimate ▶ _____ ÷ 5
 = _____

㉒ 303 ÷ 6   Estimate ▶ _____ ÷ 6
 = _____

㉓ 81 ÷ 2   Estimate ▶ _____ ÷ 2
 = _____

㉔ 804 ÷ 8   Estimate ▶ _____ ÷ 8
 = _____

㉕ 346 ÷ 7   Estimate ▶ _____ ÷ 7
 = _____

㉖ 537 ÷ 9   Estimate ▶ _____ ÷ 9
 = _____

Divide the 2-digit numbers.

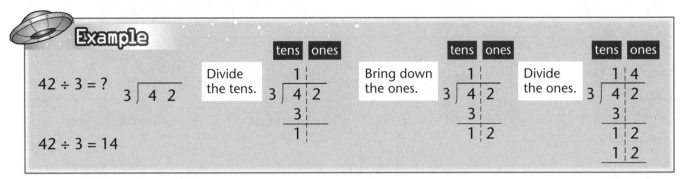

Example

$42 \div 3 = ?$

3 ⟌ 4 2

$42 \div 3 = 14$

	tens	ones
Divide the tens.

3 ⟌ 4 2
   3
   1

Bring down the ones.

3 ⟌ 4 2
   3
   1 2

Divide the ones.

3 ⟌ 4 2
   3
   1 2
   1 2

㉗   2 ⟌ 3 6

㉘   3 ⟌ 4 8

㉙   5 ⟌ 7 5

㉚   6 ⟌ 9 0

㉛ $91 \div 7 =$ _____	㉜ $96 \div 8 =$ _____	㉝ $99 \div 9 =$ _____
㉞ $74 \div 2 =$ _____	㉟ $90 \div 5 =$ _____	㊱ $84 \div 6 =$ _____
㊲ $72 \div 4 =$ _____	㊳ $75 \div 3 =$ _____	㊴ $56 \div 4 =$ _____

See how Aunt Anna put the food equally into the bags and containers. Help her find the number of things in each bag or container.

	Food	Number of bags / containers	Number of things in each bag / container
㊵	78	6	$78 \div 6 =$ _____
㊶	90	9	_____ = _____
㊷	81	3	_____ = _____
㊸	68	4	_____ = _____

Quick Tip

Round the dividend to the nearest ten to help you estimate the tens digit of the quotient.

Do the division. Write the letters representing the division sentences with remainder 2 in order. Find out what fruit Janice likes most.

㊹ 3)̄7 3 (c)	㊺ 5)̄8 4 (d)	㊻ 6)̄9 2 (o)	**Quick Tip** Quotient → ⎡1 7⎤ R ⎡1⎤ ⎡2⎤)̄⎡3 5⎤ Divisor 2 Dividend 1 5 1 4 ⎡1⎤ Remainder
㊼ 2)̄6 9 (p)	㊽ 4)̄5 3 (q)	㊾ 8)̄9 0 (r)	㊿ 7)̄8 9 (s)
51 9)̄9 2 (a)	52 6)̄8 1 (b)	53 2)̄9 5 (m)	54 5)̄9 7 (n)

55 33 ÷ 2 = ____ R ____ (f)	56 93 ÷ 7 = ____ R ____ (g)
57 55 ÷ 3 = ____ R ____ (h)	58 75 ÷ 6 = ____ R ____ (k)
59 66 ÷ 4 = ____ R ____ (e)	60 98 ÷ 8 = ____ R ____ (s)

61

I like ____ ____ ____ ____ ____ ____ ____ .

Complete the table. You can use a calculator to complete the last column.
Then answer the question.

	Division	Divisor	Quotient	Divisor x Quotient
62	5) 7 0			
63	4) 8 4			
64	3) 6 9			
65	6) 9 6			

66   What conclusion can you draw?

_____ .

Solve the problems. Show your work.

67   Ryan earned $96 in 4 weeks from delivering newspapers. How much money did he earn in one week?

_____ = _____

He earned $ _____ in one week.

68   Janice puts 92 lollipops equally into 6 jars. How many lollipops are there in each jar? How many lollipops are left behind?

_____ = _____

There are _____ lollipops in each jar. _____ lollipops are left behind.

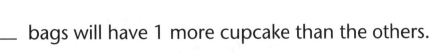

MIND BOGGLER

How many bags?

    Ryan put 95 cupcakes equally into 7 bags. He then put 1 more cupcake from the leftovers into each bag until there are no more leftovers. How many bags will have 1 more cupcake than the others?

_____ bags will have 1 more cupcake than the others.

5 Division II

Do the division.

① $4\overline{)844}$	② $3\overline{)735}$	③ $5\overline{)680}$

Quick Tip

Do the division from left to right. Round the dividend to the nearest hundred to help you estimate the hundreds digit of the quotient.

④ $564 \div 2 =$ _____

⑤ $720 \div 5 =$ _____

⑥ $928 \div 8 =$ _____

⑦ $714 \div 6 =$ _____

⑧ $672 \div 6 =$ _____

⑨ $852 \div 4 =$ _____

⑩ $975 \div 3 =$ _____

⑪ $896 \div 7 =$ _____

⑫ $791 \div 7 =$ _____

⑬ $428 \div 2 =$ _____

Divide the 3-digit numbers.

⑭ $6\overline{)186}$	⑮ $9\overline{)378}$	⑯ $7\overline{)455}$

Quick Tip

If the first digit of the 3-digit dividend is smaller than the 1-digit divisor, the quotient is a 2-digit number.

⑰ $255 \div 5 =$ _____

⑱ $288 \div 9 =$ _____

⑲ $304 \div 4 =$ _____

⑳ $252 \div 3 =$ _____

㉑ $296 \div 8 =$ _____

㉒ $186 \div 2 =$ _____

㉓ $315 \div 7 =$ _____

㉔ $396 \div 6 =$ _____

㉕ $198 \div 9 =$ _____

㉖ $240 \div 5 =$ _____

㉗ $448 \div 8 =$ _____

㉘ $273 \div 7 =$ _____

㉙ $150 \div 6 =$ _____

㉚ $666 \div 9 =$ _____

Match the division sentences with the same quotient. Help the children get their favourite toys.

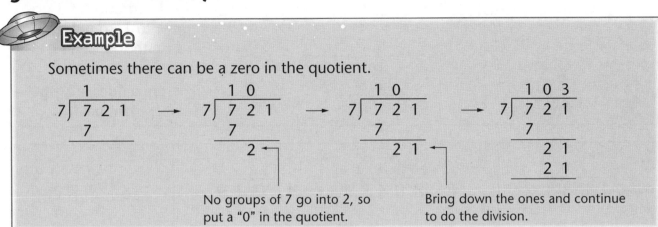

Example

Sometimes there can be a zero in the quotient.

$$
\begin{array}{r} 1 \\ 7\overline{)7\ 2\ 1} \\ 7 \\ \hline \end{array}
\quad\longrightarrow\quad
\begin{array}{r} 1\ 0 \\ 7\overline{)7\ 2\ 1} \\ 7 \\ \hline 2 \end{array}
\quad\longrightarrow\quad
\begin{array}{r} 1\ 0 \\ 7\overline{)7\ 2\ 1} \\ 7 \\ \hline 2\ 1 \end{array}
\quad\longrightarrow\quad
\begin{array}{r} 1\ 0\ 3 \\ 7\overline{)7\ 2\ 1} \\ 7 \\ \hline 2\ 1 \\ 2\ 1 \\ \hline \end{array}
$$

No groups of 7 go into 2, so put a "0" in the quotient.

Bring down the ones and continue to do the division.

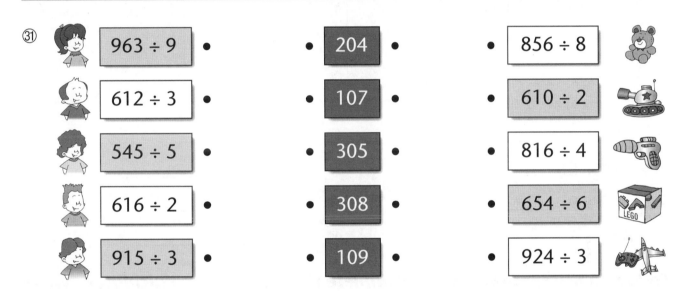

㉛

963 ÷ 9	•	•	204	•	•	856 ÷ 8
612 ÷ 3	•	•	107	•	•	610 ÷ 2
545 ÷ 5	•	•	305	•	•	816 ÷ 4
616 ÷ 2	•	•	308	•	•	654 ÷ 6
915 ÷ 3	•	•	109	•	•	924 ÷ 3

Use multiplication to check each of the following division sentences. Check ✔ the box if the quotient is correct; otherwise, write the correct quotient in the box.

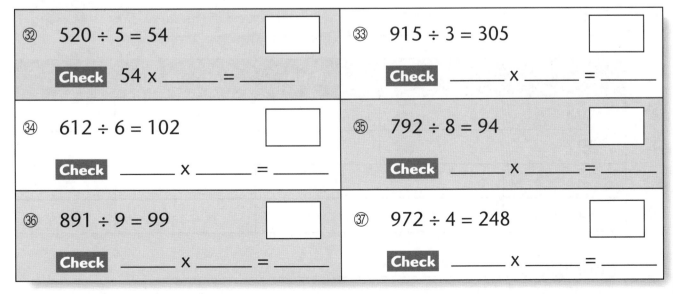

㉜ 520 ÷ 5 = 54   ☐

Check 54 x _____ = _____

㉝ 915 ÷ 3 = 305   ☐

Check _____ x _____ = _____

㉞ 612 ÷ 6 = 102   ☐

Check _____ x _____ = _____

㉟ 792 ÷ 8 = 94   ☐

Check _____ x _____ = _____

㊱ 891 ÷ 9 = 99   ☐

Check _____ x _____ = _____

㊲ 972 ÷ 4 = 248   ☐

Check _____ x _____ = _____

Do the division and use R to show the remainders.

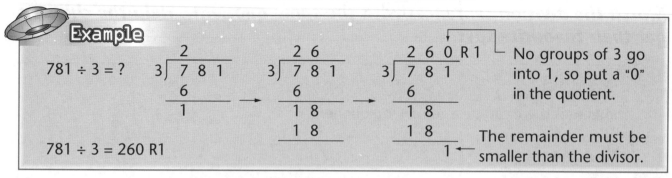

Example

$781 \div 3 = ?$

```
        2                26                2 6 0 R1        No groups of 3 go
    3) 7 8 1          3) 7 8 1          3) 7 8 1          into 1, so put a "0"
       6                 6                 6              in the quotient.
       1                 1 8               1 8
                         1 8               1 8            The remainder must be
   781 ÷ 3 = 260 R1                          1    ←       smaller than the divisor.
```

㊳	㊴	㊵	㊶
7) 6 3 1	8) 8 0 4	4) 7 7 9	6) 2 7 2

㊷ $561 \div 7 =$ _____   ㊸ $321 \div 8 =$ _____

㊹ $124 \div 5 =$ _____   ㊺ $412 \div 6 =$ _____

㊻ $425 \div 9 =$ _____   ㊼ $629 \div 4 =$ _____

㊽ $674 \div 3 =$ _____   ㊾ $741 \div 2 =$ _____

Follow Janice's instructions to complete the table with a calculator. Write a conclusion for what you can observe.

Step 1
Multiply the quotient by the divisor.

Step 2
Add the remainder to the product.

Step 3
Write down the sum in the last column of the table.

	Division	Divisor	Quotient	Remainder	Sum
㊿	405 ÷ 4				
51	397 ÷ 7				
52	721 ÷ 5				
53	643 ÷ 8				

54   Conclusion : _____

Help Uncle Tim put the stationery equally in the boxes. Check ✔ the boxes in the last column for the division with no remainders. Then circle the correct numbers.

	Number of boxes used	Number of pens in each box	Number of pens left	With or without remainder
(55) Pencils	6			
(56) Ball-points	6			
(57) Felt-pens	6			
(58) Pencils	7			
(59) Ball-points	7			
(60) Felt-pens	7			
(61) Pencils	8			
(62) Ball-points	8			
(63) Felt-pens	8			

(64) To use the smallest number of boxes without any pens left unpacked, Uncle Tim should use 6 / 7 / 8 boxes to pack the pencils, 6 / 7 / 8 boxes to pack the ball-points, and 6 / 7/ 8 boxes to pack the felt-pens.

MIND BOGGLER

How many packs ?

Uncle Tim now puts half a dozen of pencils in each box and sells them in packs of 2 boxes. How many packs of pencils are available for sale?

__________ packs are available.

6 Fractions

Janice has a bagel with white and black sesame seeds. See how Janice has cut it. Answer the questions.

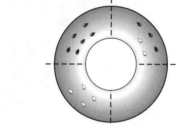

① What fraction of the bagel has sesame seeds? _____

② What fraction of the bagel has no sesame seeds? _____

③ What fraction of the bagel has black sesame seeds only? _____

④ What fraction of the bagel has both black and white sesame seeds? _____

⑤ What fraction of the sesame seeds are black? _____

⑥ What fraction of the sesame seeds are white? _____

⑦ Janice shares her bagel with her friends. What fraction of the bagel does each child have?

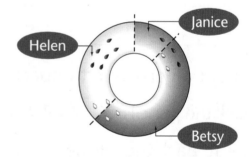

a. Janice has _____ of the bagel.

b. Betsy has _____ of the bagel.

c. Helen has _____ of the bagel.

Help Janice colour the bagels with a proper fraction green, those with an improper fraction yellow, and those with a mixed number red.

Quick Tip

Proper fraction

The numerator is smaller than the denominator, e.g. $\frac{3}{7}$.

Improper fraction

The numerator is greater than or equal to the denominator, e.g. $\frac{8}{7}, \frac{3}{3}$.

Mixed number

There is a whole number and a proper fraction, e.g. $1\frac{3}{7}$.

⑧

 $\frac{7}{9}$

 $1\frac{3}{4}$

 $\frac{8}{8}$

$\frac{8}{15}$

 $\frac{11}{10}$

 $2\frac{1}{3}$

 $\frac{1}{5}$

 $\frac{10}{6}$

 $3\frac{1}{2}$

Write the mixed number represented by each group of diagrams.

⑨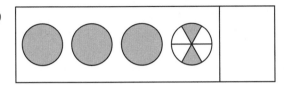

⑩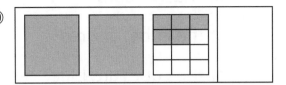

Write the improper fraction represented by each group of diagrams.

⑪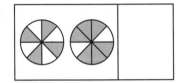

⑫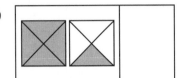

⑬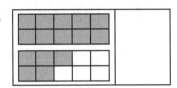

Colour the diagram to show each fraction. Then put the fractions in order from least to greatest.

⑭ a.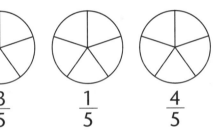

$\dfrac{3}{5}$ $\dfrac{1}{5}$ $\dfrac{4}{5}$

⑮ a.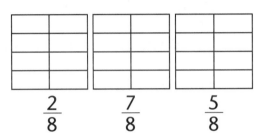

$\dfrac{2}{8}$ $\dfrac{7}{8}$ $\dfrac{5}{8}$

b. _____

b. _____

Compare the fractions. Write > or < in the boxes.

⑯ $\dfrac{7}{6}$ ☐ $\dfrac{3}{6}$

⑰ $2\dfrac{3}{8}$ ☐ $2\dfrac{5}{8}$

⑱ $3\dfrac{1}{7}$ ☐ $4\dfrac{1}{7}$

⑲ $\dfrac{8}{9}$ ☐ $\dfrac{2}{9}$

⑳ $\dfrac{5}{3}$ ☐ $\dfrac{4}{3}$

㉑ $5\dfrac{1}{10}$ ☐ $4\dfrac{1}{2}$

Put the fractions in order from greatest to least.

㉒ $\dfrac{7}{12}$ $\dfrac{13}{12}$ $\dfrac{11}{12}$ _____

㉓ $3\dfrac{1}{5}$ $3\dfrac{4}{5}$ $2\dfrac{1}{5}$ _____

Quick Tip

To compare fractions with the same denominator, compare their numerators.

e.g. $\dfrac{3}{4} > \dfrac{2}{4}$ because 3 > 2

To compare mixed numbers with the same denominator, compare the whole numbers first. If they are the same, compare their numerators.

e.g. $3\dfrac{2}{4} > 3\dfrac{1}{4}$ because 2 > 1

$5\dfrac{2}{4} > 3\dfrac{2}{4}$ because 5 > 3

Draw pictures to show each set.

㉔ Janice has 9 cubes.

$\frac{5}{9}$ of the cubes are red.

$\frac{4}{9}$ of the cubes are blue.

㉕ Danny has 15 crayons.

$\frac{6}{15}$ of the crayons are red.

$\frac{5}{15}$ of the crayons are blue.

$\frac{4}{15}$ of the crayons are green.

㉖ Uncle Tim has 12 balloons.

$\frac{3}{12}$ of the balloons are yellow.

$\frac{5}{12}$ of the balloons are blue.

The rest of the balloons are red.

Draw a set of pictures for each question to help find the missing numerator.

㉗ Aunt Anna is watering her flowers.

$\frac{5}{8}$ of her flowers are red.

$\frac{\square}{8}$ of her flowers are not red.

㉘ Some students are doing math.

$\frac{3}{5}$ of them are boys.

$\frac{\square}{5}$ of them are girls.

㉙ Pete has a box of marbles.

$\frac{3}{10}$ of the marbles are red.

$\frac{4}{10}$ of the marbles are blue.

$\frac{\square}{10}$ of the marbles are white.

Write a fraction and a decimal number to show the shaded parts in each diagram.

③⓪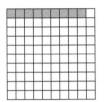

Fraction _____

Decimal _____

③①

Fraction _____

Decimal _____

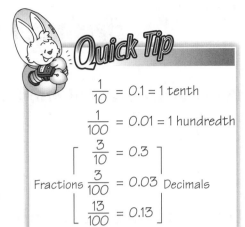

Quick Tip

$$\frac{1}{10} = 0.1 = 1 \text{ tenth}$$

$$\frac{1}{100} = 0.01 = 1 \text{ hundredth}$$

Fractions $\left[\begin{array}{l}\frac{3}{10} = 0.3 \\ \frac{3}{100} = 0.03 \\ \frac{13}{100} = 0.13\end{array}\right]$ Decimals

③②

Fraction _____

Decimal _____

③③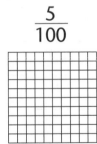

Fraction _____

Decimal _____

③④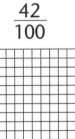

Fraction _____

Decimal _____

Colour the diagrams to show the fractions. Then write the decimals.

③⑤ $\dfrac{7}{10}$

③⑥ $\dfrac{5}{100}$

③⑦ $\dfrac{42}{100}$

_____   _____   _____

MIND BOGGLER

Draw the pictures to find the fraction.

Mom bought 12 fruits. $\dfrac{4}{12}$ of the fruits are oranges. There are 2 more apples than oranges. The rest are pears. What fraction of the fruits are pears ?

_____ of the fruits are pears.

7 Decimals

Write each decimal number in words.

①   0.2   _____

②   0.05   _____

③   0.74   _____

④   0.91   _____

Write as a decimal number.

⑤   Four tenths   _____

⑥   Eight hundredths   _____

⑦   Twelve hundredths   _____

⑧   Sixty-seven hundredths   _____

Write each decimal number on the place value chart.

		tens	ones	tenths	hundredths
⑨	5.2				
⑩	7.49				
⑪	58.1				

Write the place value and meaning of each underlined digit.

⑫   2.4<u>6</u>   place value _____   means _____

⑬   1.<u>4</u>2   place value _____   means _____

⑭   <u>7</u>.12   place value _____   means _____

⑮   8.5<u>9</u>   place value _____   means _____

Help Janice compare the prices of candies in two stores. Write > or < in the boxes.

⑯ $0.42 ☐ $0.39   ⑰ $2.15 ☐ $2.24

⑱ $0.87 ☐ $1.01   ⑲ $1.03 ☐ $1.30

Write the numbers in order from least to greatest.

⑳   0.1   0.07   1.4   _____

㉑   2.20   2.02   20.2   _____

㉒   3.42   3.04   4.32   _____

Use the number line below to help round the decimals to the nearest whole number.

Examples

①   2.3 is between 2 and 3 , and it is closer to 2. Therefore 2.3 is rounded to 2.
②   1.5 is midway between 1 and 2. It should be rounded up to 2.

㉓   3.7   _____   ㉔   0.8   _____   ㉕   2.9   _____

㉖   1.2   _____   ㉗   3.1   _____   ㉘   3.5   _____

Write the decimals and complete the addition or subtraction sentences to match the pictures.

㉙ 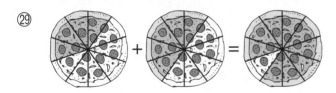   ㉚

_____ + _____ = _____   _____ + _____ = _____

㉛ 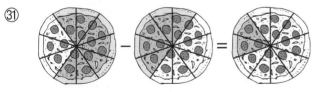   ㉜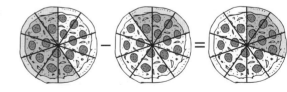

_____ − _____ = _____   _____ − _____ = _____

㉝

_____ + _____ = _____

Do the addition.

Quick Tip

Align the decimal points when doing vertical addition or subtraction. Then add or subtract as with whole numbers. Remember to put a decimal point in the answer directly under the decimal points above.

㉞
```
    0.9
+   1.4
```

㉟
```
    2.5
+   1.3
```

㊱
```
  2 3.7
+    2.6
```

㊲
```
  5 4.1
+ 1 0.8
```

㊳
```
    7.2
+ 1 1.8
```

㊴
```
  1 0.3
+    6.5
```

㊵ 8.7 + 41.9 = _____

㊶ 15.8 + 10.6 = _____

㊷ 12.4 + 76.3 = _____

㊸ 37.9 + 3.2 = _____

㊹ 50.8 + 35.6 = _____

㊺ 101.5 + 24.7 = _____

Do the subtraction.

㊻
```
    8.7
-   2.5
```

㊼
```
    7.3
-   0.9
```

㊽
```
  1 2.4
-    9.6
```

㊾
```
  2 0.1
- 1 7.2
```

㊿
```
  1 3.4
-    5.9
```

51
```
  2 6.7
- 1 6.8
```

52
```
  4 9.9
- 2 4.6
```

53
```
  7 6.9
- 2 9.3
```

54 71.8 – 10.9 = _____

55 119.1 – 28.6 = _____

56 68.4 – 15.7 = _____

57 103.1 – 41.7 = _____

Estimate each answer by rounding the decimals to the nearest whole number. Then find the exact answer.

58
```
  1 2.3  ⟶
+ 2 6.9  ⟶      +  _____
```

59
```
  4 2.8  ⟶
- 1 7.9  ⟶      –  _____
```

Look at the locations of the children's homes and solve the problems.

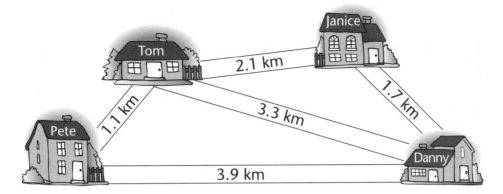

⑥⓪ Tom went to meet Janice at her house. Then he walked to Danny's home. How many km did Tom walk altogether?

_____ = _____   _____ km altogether

⑥① If Tom goes directly to Danny's house, by how many km will the route be shorter?

_____ = _____   _____ km

⑥② How many km does Pete walk if he goes to Danny's house via Tom's house?

_____ = _____   _____ km

⑥③ How many more km will Pete walk if he goes by the route in ⑥② instead of the direct route?

_____ = _____   _____ km more

MIND BOGGLER

Fill in the names and complete the sentence.

Janice is going to give each of her three friends an apple pie. She will walk to her friends' houses and her father will drive her home later. Janice wants to take the shortest route to deliver the apple pies.

The shortest route is :

The total distance Janice has to walk is _____ km.

Progress Test

Complete the table to show the place value and the meaning of the grey digit in each number.

Number	0.5**3**	**4**230	**2**1.7	6.**1**9	**7**528
① Place value					
② Meaning					

Write the numbers.

③   6 thousands 3 hundreds 5 tens   _____

④   Seven thousand eight hundred twenty-nine   _____

⑤   Forty-two hundredths   _____

⑥   Two thousand three   _____

⑦   36 and 9 hundredths   _____

Write each number in words.

⑧   25.13   _____

⑨   0.07   _____

⑩   0.9   _____

⑪   4028   _____

⑫   7506   _____

Fill in the correct numbers.

⑬   6793   = 6000 + _____ + _____ + _____

⑭   3075   = _____ thousands _____ hundreds _____ tens _____ ones

⑮   _____ = 5000 + 80 + 9

⑯   _____ = 4 thousands 6 hundreds 5 ones

⑰   _____ = 3 tens and 19 hundredths

Fill in the missing numbers.

⑱   4913   5093   _____   _____   5393   _____

⑲   9080   _____   7080   _____   _____   4080

⑳   0.19   0.29   _____   0.59   _____

Put the numbers in order.

㉑   1.3   1.03   1.33   _____ > _____ > _____

㉒   5.46   5.64   5.06   _____ > _____ > _____

㉓   8736   9736   8973   _____ < _____ < _____

㉔ $\frac{11}{15}$ $\frac{17}{15}$ $\frac{3}{15}$ $\frac{9}{15}$ _____ < _____ < _____ < _____

㉕ $2\frac{3}{9}$ $2\frac{7}{9}$ $1\frac{3}{9}$ $1\frac{1}{9}$ _____ > _____ > _____ > _____

Write a fraction and a decimal number for the shaded parts of the diagram in ㉖ and colour the diagrams to show the fractions or decimal numbers in ㉗ and ㉘. Fill in the missing numbers.

㉖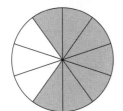

Fraction _____

Decimal _____

㉗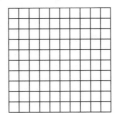

Fraction $\frac{79}{100}$

Decimal _____

㉘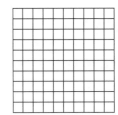

Fraction _____

Decimal 0.06

Fill in the boxes with 'P' to represent proper fractions, 'I' to represent improper fractions, and 'M' to represent mixed numbers.

㉙ $\frac{14}{14}$ ☐   ㉚ $3\frac{6}{9}$ ☐   ㉛ $\frac{7}{18}$ ☐   ㉜ $\frac{17}{11}$ ☐

㉝ $5\frac{7}{12}$ ☐   ㉞ $\frac{15}{8}$ ☐   ㉟ $\frac{4}{7}$ ☐   ㊱ $\frac{9}{13}$ ☐

Calculate.

�37 6 4 7 3 − 9 4 8	㊳ 3 6 x 9	㊴ 9 4 3 x 8	㊵ 2 5 6 4 + 4 7 9 5
㊶ 4 ⟌ 2 4 3	㊷ 5 ⟌ 8 6	㊸ 6 ⟌ 7 5 6	㊹ 7 ⟌ 2 4 8
㊺ 3.6 + 2 1.8	㊻ 3 9.5 + 1 6.4	㊼ 4 6.9 − 2.7	㊽ 2 3.4 − 1 9.8

㊾ 9.2 + 45.9 = _____

㊿ 23.1 − 9.8 = _____

(51) 72 x 6 = _____

(52) 805 x 7 = _____

(53) 96 ÷ 8 = _____

(54) 864 ÷ 8 = _____

(55) 542 x 6 = _____

(56) 7203 − 874 = _____

Draw pictures to help complete the sentences.

(57) Janice has a collection of ♡ stickers.

$\frac{3}{12}$ of the stickers are red. $\frac{4}{12}$ of the stickers

are blue. The rest are yellow.

a. $\frac{}{12}$ of the stickers are yellow.

b. Most of the stickers are _____ .

c. _____ stickers are the fewest.

36

The children are playing computer games. Help them solve the problems.

⑤⑧ Sam scored 3468 points in 6 rounds. If he got the same points in each round, what was his score in each round?

_____ = _____

His score in each round was _____ points.

⑤⑨ Sam scored 1020 points in the 7th round. What was his total score in 7 rounds?

_____ = _____

His total score in 7 rounds was _____ points.

⑥⓪ Edith scored 615 points fewer than Sam. What was her total score?

_____ = _____

Her total score was _____ points.

⑥① Tom scored 837 points in each of the first 4 rounds. What was his total score in the first 4 rounds?

_____ = _____

His total score in the first 4 rounds was _____ points.

⑥② Sam took 1.2 hours to finish the first 6 rounds and 0.4 hour to finish the 7th round. How much time did he use to finish the game?

_____ = _____

He used _____ hours to finish the game.

⑥③ Tom took 0.5 hour more than Sam to finish the game and Edith took 0.2 hour less than Tom. How long did Edith take to finish the game?

_____ = _____

Edith took _____ hours to finish the game.

8 Geometry I

Identify each set of lines and write the letter in the box.

| A | parallel lines | B | perpendicular lines | C | intersecting lines |

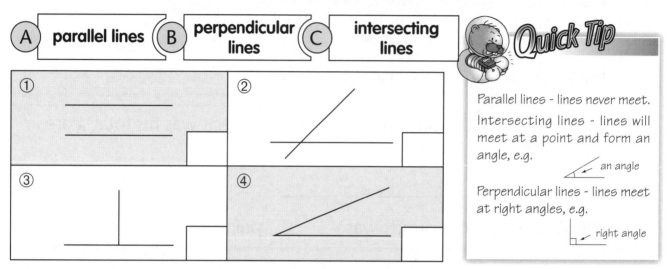

Quick Tip

Parallel lines - lines never meet.

Intersecting lines - lines will meet at a point and form an angle, e.g. ___ an angle

Perpendicular lines - lines meet at right angles, e.g. ___ right angle

Identify the angles formed by the clock hands. Write their representing letters in the right boxes.

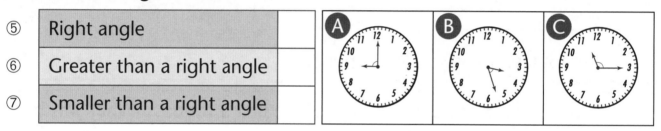

⑤	Right angle	
⑥	Greater than a right angle	
⑦	Smaller than a right angle	

Measure the following angles using a protractor.

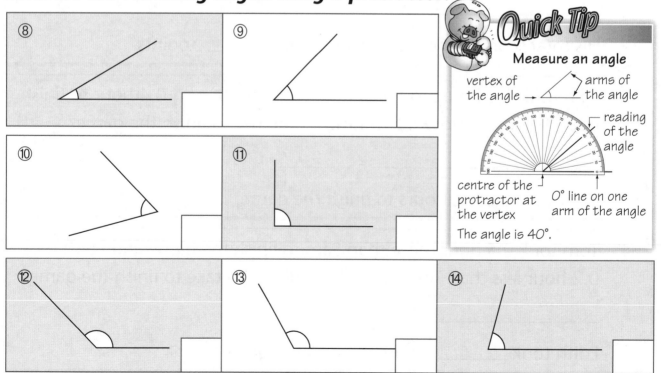

Quick Tip

Measure an angle

vertex of the angle → ___ arms of the angle

reading of the angle

centre of the protractor at the vertex

0° line on one arm of the angle

The angle is 40°.

38

Colour the quadrilaterals.

⑮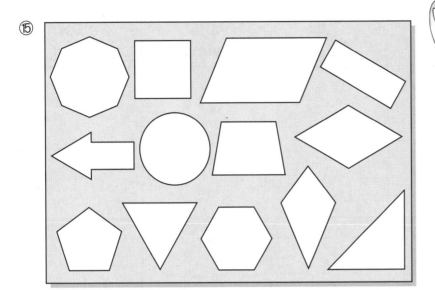

Write the name of each shape. Then check ✔ the boxes to show its properties.

⑯ A   B   C   D   E

_____   _____   _____   _____   _____

Property	Shape	A	B	C	D	E
⑰ 4 equal sides						
⑱ 2 pairs of equal sides						
⑲ 2 pairs of parallel sides						
⑳ 1 pair of parallel sides only						
㉑ 4 right angles						

What shapes are they? Write their names in the boxes.

㉒ It has 2 pairs of equal sides and 4 right angles.

㉓ It has 2 pairs of parallel sides and all sides are equal.

㉔ It has only 1 pair of parallel sides.

㉕ It has 2 pairs of equal sides and no right angles.

㉖ It has 4 equal sides and 4 right angles.

Write the name of each shape and sketch its faces.

Shape / Name	Front View	Top View	Side View	Bottom View
㉗				
㉘				
㉙				

Janice makes the skeletons of some 3-D shapes with straws and marshmallows. Help her complete the skeletons and fill in the missing numbers.

Name	Skeleton	Number of edges or vertices
㉚ Cube		edges
		vertices
㉛ Pentagonal pyramid		edges
		vertices

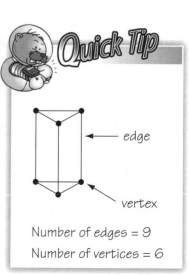

Quick Tip

edge

vertex

Number of edges = 9
Number of vertices = 6

Find the congruent and similar shapes. Write the letters in the right boxes.

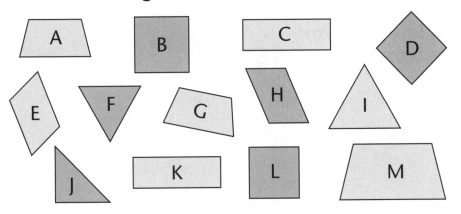

③② | Congruent pairs

③③ | Similar pairs

Draw a similar figure and a congruent figure for the shape.

③④

MIND BOGGLER

Use the geoboard to help you draw a congruent figure of the 3-D shape.

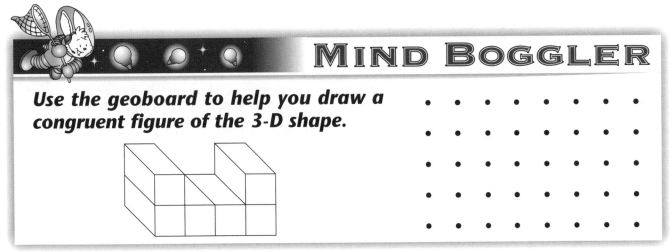

9 Units of Measure

Write the most appropriate unit you would use to measure each object.

① Your pencil _____

② Distance from home to school _____

③ Your height _____

④ The height of the door _____   ⑤ A worm _____

⑥ Your desk _____   ⑦ An ant _____

Janice has several pencils. Help her measure the length of each pencil in mm. Then write the length in cm.

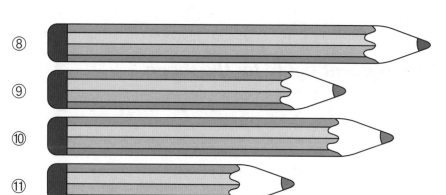

⑧

⑨

⑩

⑪

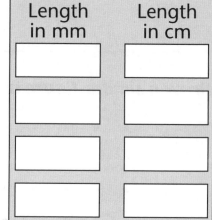

Length in mm	Length in cm

Draw pictures following the instructions.

⑫ Draw a foot 5 cm long.	⑬ Draw a butterfly 30 mm wide.
⑭ Draw a button 12 mm wide.	⑮ Draw a paper clip 33 mm long and 8 mm wide.

Janice was celebrating her tenth birthday with her friends. Help the children fill in the missing numbers in the game card.

⑯ 20 years are _____ decades.

⑰ 500 years are _____ centuries.

⑱ 3000 years are _____ millenniums.

⑲ 800 years are _____ decades.

⑳ There are _____ years in half a century.

㉑ There are _____ years in a quarter of a millennium.

㉒ Canada was 134 years old in the year 2001. Her age was _____ century _____ decades and _____ years.

Quick Tip

1 decade = 10 years
1 century = 100 years or 10 decades
1 millennium = 1000 years or 100 decades

The children were playing computer games. See when each child started and finished the game. Complete the table and sentences.

㉓	Janice	Pete	Marie	Joey	Tom	Sam
Starting time	2:29	2:54	3:27	3:58	4:18	4:50
Finishing time	2:54	3:27	3:58	4:18	4:50	5:20
Time used (min)						

㉔ _____ used the shortest time to finish the game.

㉕ _____ used the longest time to finish the game.

㉖ Janice used _____ min longer than Joey.

㉗ Sam used 1 min shorter than _____ .

㉘ Time used by Joey and _____ differed by 10 min.

㉙ Time used by _____ and _____ differed by 3 min.

Quick Tip

To determine time intervals, trade 1 hour for 60 minutes if necessary, e.g. the time interval between 2:12 and 1:49 can be calculated by

$$\begin{array}{r} 1:72 \\ -1:49 \\ \hline 23 \end{array}$$

Time interval is 23 min.

The children were each given $50 to buy their favourite toys. See what they bought and write the change they got in the boxes. Then answer the questions.

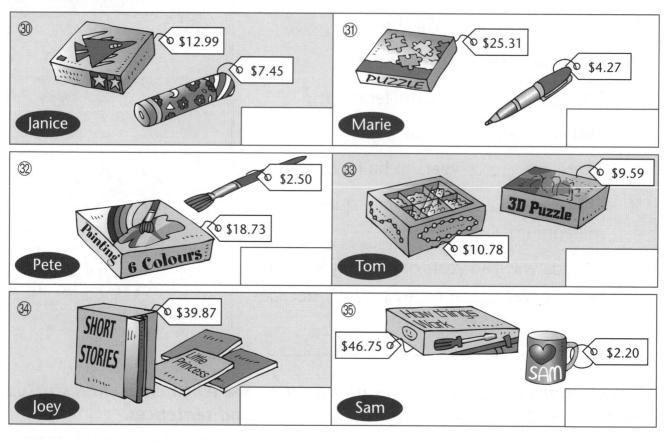

③⓪ Janice — $12.99, $7.45

③① Marie — $25.31, $4.27

③② Pete — $2.50, $18.73

③③ Tom — $9.59, $10.78

③④ Joey — $39.87

③⑤ Sam — $46.75, $2.20

③⑥ Who spent the most money? _____

③⑦ Who got the most change? _____

The numbers of bills and coins are shown in the circles. Find the total amount in each group.

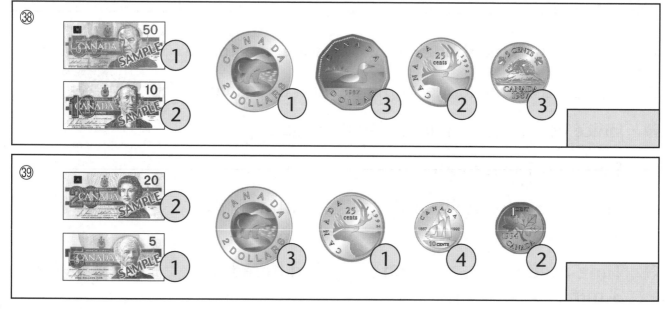

Look at the prices and help the children solve the problems. Show your work.

$14.63 $35.49 $8.51 $26.37

40 Anna has $35. She wants to buy the snow globe and one other item. Which item can she buy?

She can buy the _____ .

41 Calvin has $50. Does he have enough money to buy the clock and the table lamp?

He _____ enough money to buy both items.

42 Michelle has $40. If she wants to buy the table lamp and the photo frame, how much more money does she need?

She needs $ _____ more.

43 Julie has $50 and she wants to buy as many items as she can. Which items can she buy?

She can buy _____

_____ .

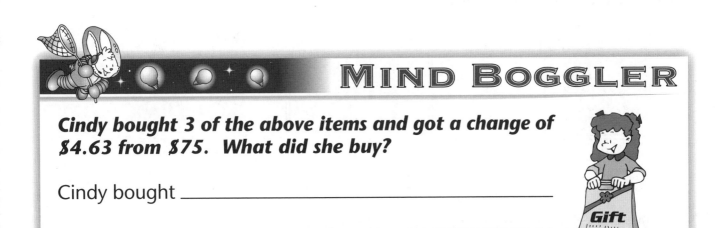

MIND BOGGLER

Cindy bought 3 of the above items and got a change of $4.63 from $75. What did she buy?

Cindy bought _____

_____ .

⑩ **Perimeter and Area**

Check ✔ the circle to show whether you would consider the 'perimeter' or 'area' in each case. Then select the most appropriate unit of measure. Write cm, m, cm², or m² on the line.

① The carpet for covering the floor of the family room

　　◯ perimeter　　◯ area　　_____

② The flower chain for decorating the tack board

　　◯ perimeter　　◯ area　　_____

③ The fencing around the backyard

　　◯ perimeter　　◯ area　　_____

④ The treated planks for building a deck

　　◯ perimeter　　◯ area　　_____

⑤ The decorating paper for wrapping up a storybook

　　◯ perimeter　　◯ area　　_____

> **Quick Tip**
>
> Centimetres (cm) and square centimetres (cm²) are for measuring the perimeter and area of a small thing. Metres (m) and square metres (m²) are for measuring a large thing.

Help Janice measure the sides and find the perimeter (P) of each sticker. Then answer the questions.

⑥

P = _____ cm

⑦

P = _____ cm

⑧

P = _____ cm

⑨ Which sticker has the greatest perimeter?　　_____

⑩ Which sticker has the least perimeter?　　_____

Janice cut out different shapes for her art project. Help her calculate the perimeter of each shape.

⑪	Perimeter
A	
B	
C	
D	
E	
F	

Shape A: 4 cm (top), 5 cm (left), 4 cm (bottom), 3 cm, 3 cm

Shape B: 2 cm (top), 4 cm, 8 cm (left), 2 cm, 4 cm, 4 cm, 4 cm (bottom)

Shape C: 5 cm (top), 8 cm (left), 8 cm (right), 5 cm (bottom)

Shape D: 15 cm (top), 8 cm, 8 cm (right), 8 cm, 15 cm (bottom), 8 cm (left)

Shape E: 4 cm (top), 2 cm, 3 cm, 2 cm, 5 cm, 6 cm (left), 2 cm, 6 cm (bottom)

Shape F: 10 cm, 12 cm, 14 cm

Pete drew some shapes on the centimetre grid paper. Help him find the perimeter and area of each shape.

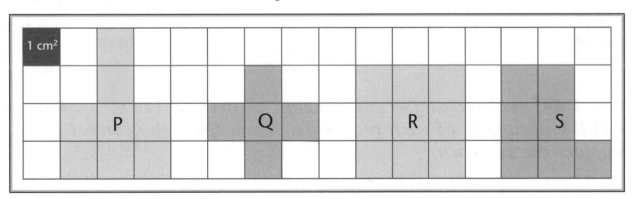

1 cm²   P   Q   R   S

	P	Q	R	S
⑫	Perimeter				
⑬	Area				

⑭   Which shape has the greatest perimeter? _____

⑮   Which shape has the greatest area? _____

⑯   Does the shape with the greatest perimeter have

the greatest area? _____

Estimate the area of each polygon on the centimetre grid paper.

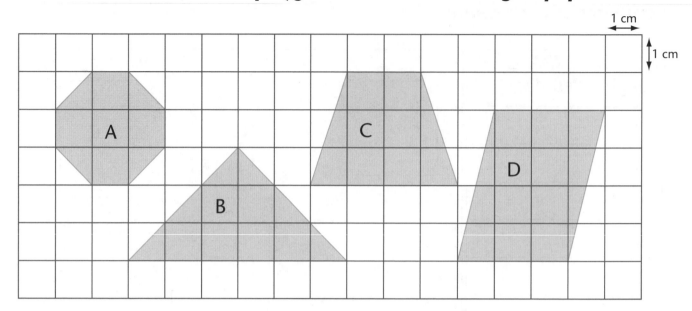

⑰	A	
⑱	B	
⑲	C	
⑳	D	

Quick Tip

Count each ▣ as 1 cm². Count each ▯ or ◿ as 0.5 cm². Count each part greater than ▯ or ◿ as 1 cm². Do not count the squares with less than half shaded.

Draw 3 different rectangles each having an area of 12 cm². Count and label the perimeter of each rectangle. Then circle the correct word to complete the sentence.

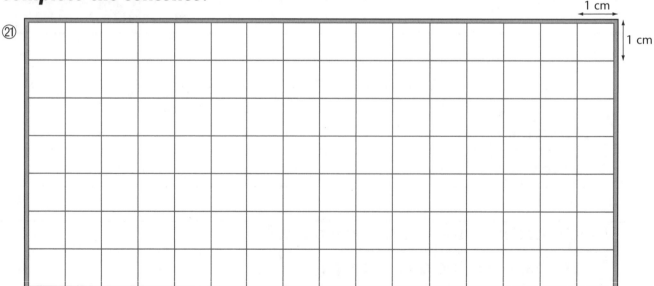

⑳ The perimeters of the rectangles are the same / different .

Draw 3 different shapes each having a perimeter of 16 cm on the centimetre dot paper. Count and label the area of each shape. Then circle the correct word to complete the sentence.

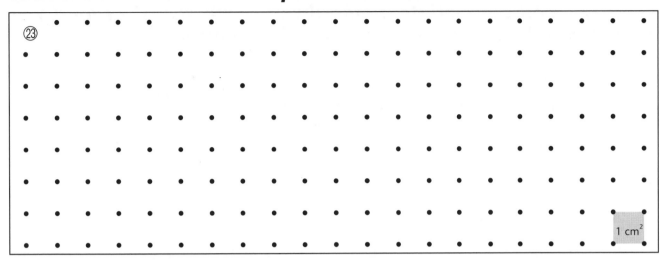

㉔   The areas of the shapes are the same / different .

MIND BOGGLER

Draw Marie's bookmarks.

Marie has designed a rectangular bookmark with an area of 27 cm^2 and a perimeter of 24 cm. Help her design and draw 2 more bookmarks so that one has a greater area but a smaller perimeter than A while the other has a smaller area but a greater perimeter than A. Label the area and the perimeter of each bookmark.

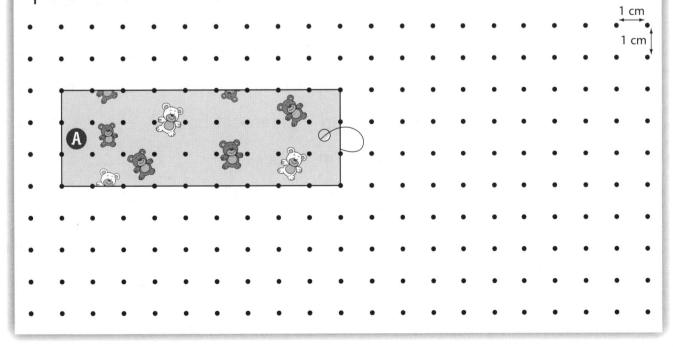

11 Capacity, Volume, and Mass

Select the most appropriate standard unit to measure the capacity of each of the following containers. Write litre or millilitre.

① A swimming pool _____

② A big fish tank _____

③ An eyedrop bottle _____

④ A medicine bottle _____

⑤ A syringe _____

⑥ A teaspoon _____

⑧ A bathtub _____

⑩ A mug _____

⑦ The gas tank of a car _____

⑨ A bucket _____

⑪ A garbage can _____

> **Quick Tip**
>
> Capacity is the amount of liquid a container can hold. It is measured in litres (L) or millilitres (mL). Litres measure larger capacities and millilitres measure smaller capacities.
>
> 1 L = 1000 mL

Pete is comparing the capacity of the containers he found at home. Look at the containers and answer the questions.

 250 mL

 Milk 1 L

 Detergent 750 mL

 Syrup 500 mL

 3 L

⑫ How many mugs of water can fill up 1 milk carton? _____ mugs

⑬ How many bottles of syrup can fill up 1 milk carton? _____ bottles

⑭ How many mugs of water can fill up 1 detergent bottle? _____ mugs

⑮ How many cartons of milk can fill up 1 bucket? _____ cartons

⑯ How many bottles of syrup can fill up 1 bucket? _____ bottles

⑰ How many bottles of detergent can fill up 1 bucket? _____ bottles

⑱ List the containers in order from the one with least capacity to the one with greatest.

Michelle uses centimetre cubes to build the following structures. Count the number of cubes used to determine the volume of each structure.

⑲

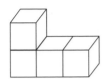

Volume : _____

⑳

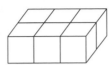

Volume : _____

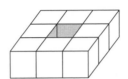
Quick Tip

Volume is the amount of space an object occupies.

A centimetre cube is a cube with length, width, and heigth of 1 cm.

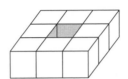
1cm
1cm
1cm

The volume of a centimetre cube is 1 cubic centimetre (cm^3).

㉑

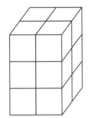

Volume : _____

㉒

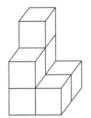

Volume : _____

㉓

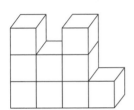

Volume : _____

㉔

Volume : _____

㉕

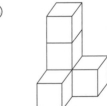

Volume : _____

Use 16 centimetre cubes to build 2 different prisms. Draw them and answer the questions.

㉖ a.

Prism A	Prism B

b. Do the prisms have the same volume? _____

c. Do the prisms have the same height? _____

d. Do the prisms have the same width? _____

Select the most appropriate standard unit to measure the mass of each of the following items. Write kilogram, gram, or milligram.

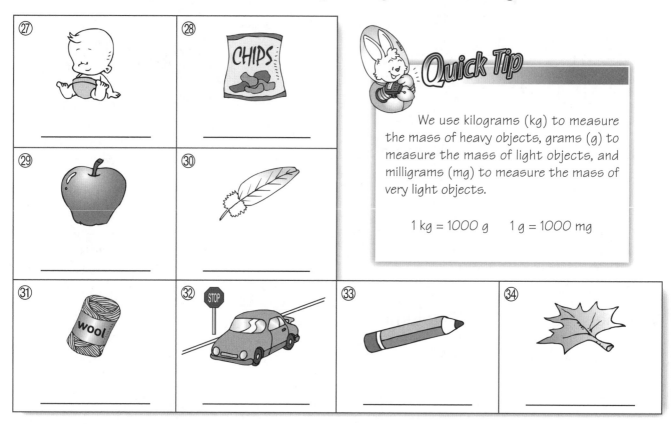

㉗ _____

㉘ _____

㉙ _____

㉚ _____

Quick Tip

We use kilograms (kg) to measure the mass of heavy objects, grams (g) to measure the mass of light objects, and milligrams (mg) to measure the mass of very light objects.

1 kg = 1000 g   1 g = 1000 mg

㉛ _____

㉜ _____

㉝ _____

㉞ _____

Answer the questions.

Potatoes 10 kg   Cornflakes 550 g   Sausages 950 g   Black Pepper 55 g   750 g

㉟   How much heavier are the sausages than the cornflakes?   _____

㊱   Which food is 200 g lighter than the bananas?   _____

㊲   Which thing has a mass closest to 1 kg?   _____

㊳   Which thing has a mass closest to 0.1 kg?   _____

㊴   Which food is 10 times as heavy as the black pepper?   _____

㊵   What is the mass of 1 banana?   _____

㊶   List the masses in order from heaviest to lightest.

_____

Check ✔ the most reasonable estimate for the mass of each item.

㊷ a loonie

A less than 10 g	B 10 to 50 g	C over 50 g

㊸ an adult

A less than 40 kg	B 40 to 100 kg	C over 150 kg

㊹ a piano

A less than 100 kg	B 100 to 250 kg	C over 250 kg

Circle the correct mass in each question.

㊺	The greater mass	3.5 kg	or	350 g
㊻	The lighter mass	1 kg	or	900 g
㊼	The mass that is closer to 2 kg	2100 g	or	1800 g

Janice has written some sentences about her things. Help her make each sentence reasonable by filling in kg, g, or mg.

㊽ My mass is about 30 000 ____ .

㊾ The bit of nail clipped from my thumb is about 20 ____ .

㊿ I have a table tennis ball of mass about 2 ____ .

(51) Yesterday, I bought a 1- ____ bag of sugar for Mom.

MIND BOGGLER

Look at the pictograph that shows the masses of different animals compared with the average mass of a man. Answer the questions.

① How many pigs will weigh the same as a horse? ________

② What is the smallest number of calves, pigs, and tigers together to weigh as a horse?

____

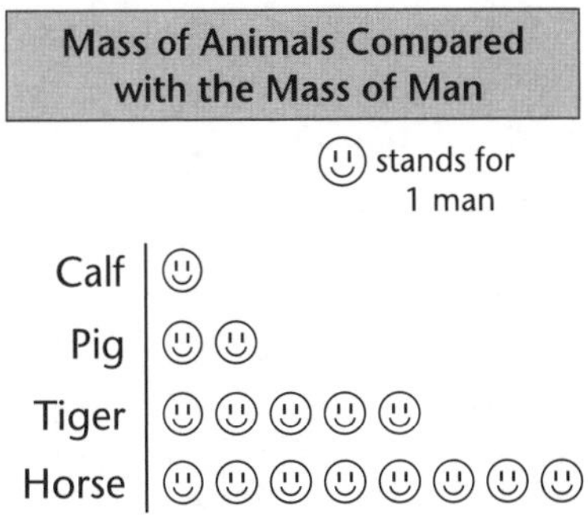
Mass of Animals Compared with the Mass of Man
☺ stands for 1 man
Calf
Pig
Tiger
Horse

Geometry II

Describe the transformations with 'Translation', 'Reflection', or 'Rotation'.

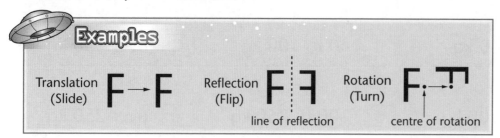

Transformation

The change of position and orientation of an object

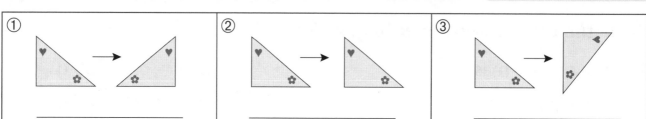

Draw the reflection images of these letters.

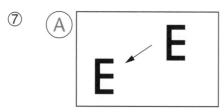

Which diagrams below each shows a translation? Check ✔ the letter.

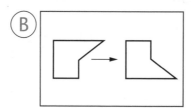

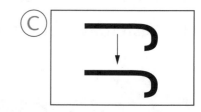

In each set, check ✔ the one that shows a rotation image of the shape on the left.

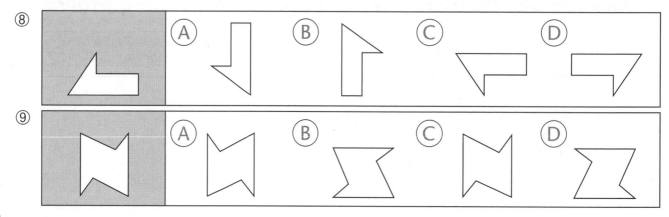

Draw an image of each shape for each type of transformation.

		Translation	Reflection	Rotation
⑩		a.	b.	c.
⑪		a.	b.	c.

Describe how the shape is translated in each case. Write the numbers and circle the correct words.

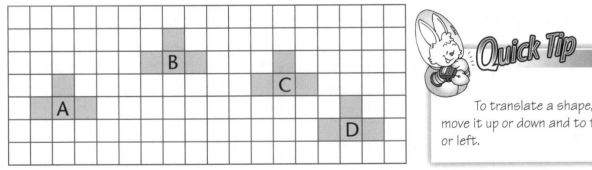

> **Quick Tip**
>
> To translate a shape, you can move it up or down and to the right or left.

⑫ A ➜ B   ____ square(s) up / down and ____ square(s) left / right

⑬ B ➜ D   ____ square(s) up / down and ____ square(s) left / right

⑭ D ➜ C   ____ square(s) up / down and ____ square(s) left / right

⑮ C ➜ A   ____ square(s) up / down and ____ square(s) left / right

Write 'quarter', 'half', or 'full' to show how the letter 'Q' is rotated in a clockwise direction.

⑯

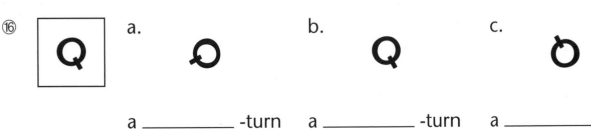

a.   b.   c.

a _____ -turn   a _____ -turn   a _____ -turn

Use a ruler to draw the lines of symmetry.

⑰

Complete the symmetrical diagrams. (↔) represents the line of symmetry.

⑱

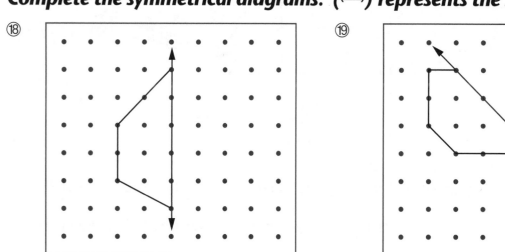

⑲

⑳

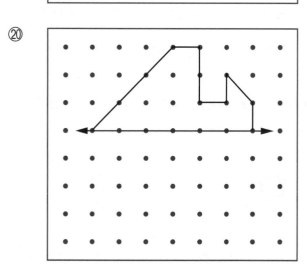

㉑

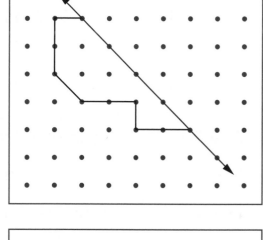

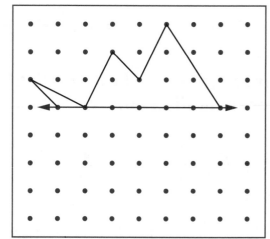

Sam is in Ferns Park. Look at the map and guide him through the Park.

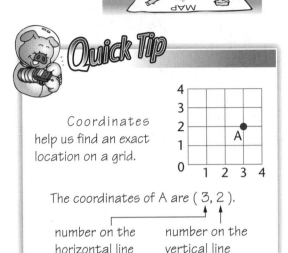

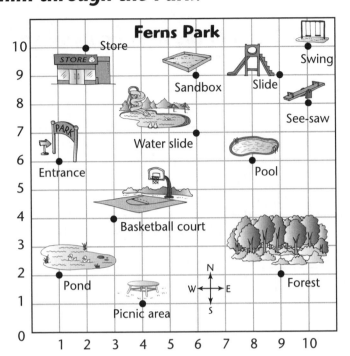

Ferns Park

10 Store
9
8
7 PARK
6 Entrance
5
4 Basketball court
3
2 Pond
1 Picnic area
0   1 2 3 4 5 6 7 8 9 10

Swing
Sandbox   Slide
See-saw
Water slide
Pool
Forest

N
W — E
S

Quick Tip

Coordinates help us find an exact location on a grid.

4
3
2 A
1
0
  1 2 3 4

The coordinates of A are (3 , 2).

number on the horizontal line   number on the vertical line

㉒ Write the coordinates of the following locations.

a. Entrance   (___ , ___)   b. Slide   (___ , ___)

c. Picnic area   (___ , ___)   d. See-saw   (___ , ___)

e. Swing   (___ , ___)   f. Forest   (___ , ___)

㉓ Read the coordinates and write the locations.

a. (8 , 6) _____   b. (1 , 2) _____

c. (6 , 7) _____   d. (2 , 10) _____

e. (3 , 4) _____   f. (6 , 9) _____

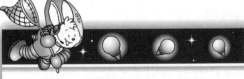

MIND BOGGLER

Look at the map above and find out Sam's route. Write the places he passed by.

Sam started from the entrance and walked 4 units south to A, 3 units east and 1 unit south to B, and finally 4 units east and 5 units north to C.

Sam's route : Entrance → _____ → _____ → _____

13 Patterns and Simple Equations

Continue each skip counting pattern by filling in the missing numbers.

①	12	15	18	21				
②	44	48	52	56				
③	70	65	60			45		
④	60	54	48			30		
⑤	14	21	28			49		
⑥	8	16	24				56	
⑦	90	81	72	63				
⑧	20	30			60		80	

Draw the next two shapes in each pattern.

⑨

⑩

⑪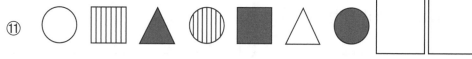

⑫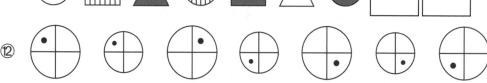

Quick Tip

There may be changes in two or more attributes of the shapes, e.g. size, shape, orientation, pattern.

Look for the patterns and complete the sentences.

⑬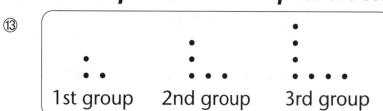

1st group   2nd group   3rd group

There will be _____ •
in the 5th group.

⑭

```
                    x x x
          x x       x x x
    x     x x       x x x
```
1st group   2nd group   3rd group

There will be _____ x
in the 6th group.

Finish each number pattern by writing the next 3 numbers. Then give the rule of each pattern.

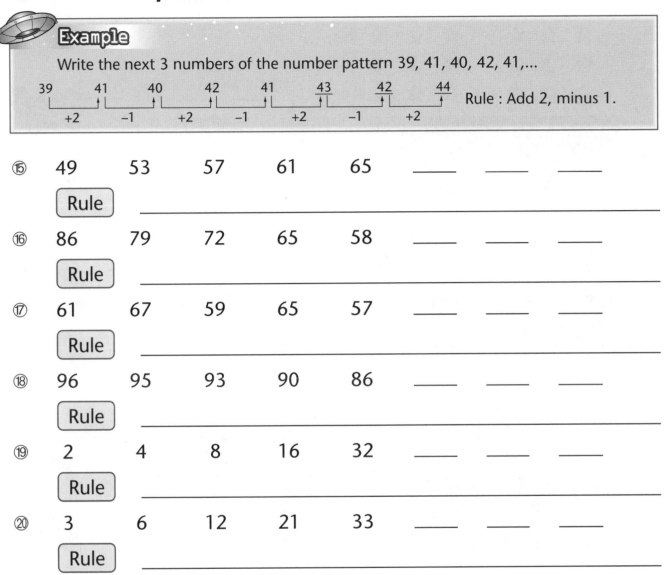

Example

Write the next 3 numbers of the number pattern 39, 41, 40, 42, 41,...

39   41   40   42   41   43   42   44   Rule : Add 2, minus 1.
     +2   −1   +2   −1   +2   −1   +2

⑮   49   53   57   61   65   _____   _____   _____

   Rule _____

⑯   86   79   72   65   58   _____   _____   _____

   Rule _____

⑰   61   67   59   65   57   _____   _____   _____

   Rule _____

⑱   96   95   93   90   86   _____   _____   _____

   Rule _____

⑲   2   4   8   16   32   _____   _____   _____

   Rule _____

⑳   3   6   12   21   33   _____   _____   _____

   Rule _____

Complete the table to show the pattern and solve the problem.

㉑   Joanne baked 7 cookies and 3 doughnuts on Monday, 10 cookies and 6 doughnuts on Tuseday, and 13 cookies and 9 doughnuts on Wednesday. Following this pattern, how many cookies and doughnuts did she bake on Friday?

a.

	Monday	Tuesday	Wednesday	Thursday	Friday
No. of cookies					
No. of doughnuts					

b. Joanne baked _____ cookies and _____ doughnuts on Friday.

Ms. Beatty's class sew duvet covers to raise money for the Children Cancer Fund. Look at the designs and complete the tables.

㉒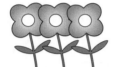

I like the night sky.

Number of moons	1	2	3	4	5	6
Number of stars	8	10				

㉓

I like flowers.

Number of stalks	1	2	3	4	5	6
Number of petals	4	8				

㉔

I like monsters, but I don't know how to sew a duvet cover.

Number of eyes	2	3	4	5	6	7
Number of legs	2	4				

㉕

I am able to sew a very simple pattern only.

Number of squares	1	2	3	4	5	6
Number of triangles	3	4				

㉖

I use squares to make diamonds.

Number of diamonds	1	2	3	4	5	6
Number of squares						

Complete the number sentences so that the answers are the same on both sides of each balance. You may use a calculator.

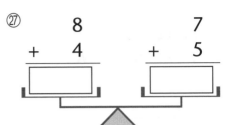

㉗

$$8 + 4 = \boxed{} \qquad 7 + 5 = \boxed{}$$

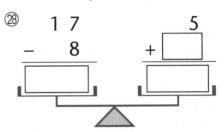

㉘

$$1\ 7 - 8 = \boxed{} \qquad \boxed{} + 5 = \boxed{}$$

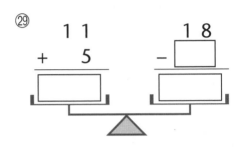

㉙

$$1\ 1 + 5 = \boxed{} \qquad 1\ 8 - \boxed{} = \boxed{}$$

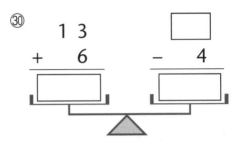

㉚

$$1\ 3 + 6 = \boxed{} \qquad \boxed{} - 4 = \boxed{}$$

Determine the missing term in each equation. You can use the 'guess-and-test' method or a calculator.

㉛ $63 = 60 + \blacksquare$

$\blacksquare =$ _____

㉜ $37 = 42 - \blacktriangle$

$\blacktriangle =$ _____

㉝ $2 + 3 + 5 = 16 - \heartsuit$

$\heartsuit =$ _____

㉞ $12 - 8 = \clubsuit + 3$

$\clubsuit =$ _____

㉟ $a + 7 = 12 + 18$

$a =$ _____

㊱ $b - 6 = 20 - 10$

$b =$ _____

㊲ $c - 10 = 16 + 9$

$c =$ _____

㊳ $d + 2 = 25 - 20$

$d =$ _____

MIND BOGGLER

Fill in the missing numbers.

①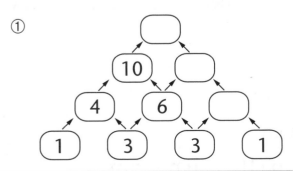

②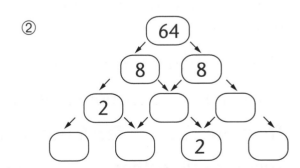

14 Graphs and Probability

Ms. Beatty's class is visiting Uncle Tim's farm. Uncle Tim uses a pictograph to show the children the type and number of animals on his farm. Read the graph to find the answers.

① Tally the number of animals.

Pig	Horse	Cow	Hen	Sheep	Duck

Quick Tip

Remember that each tally mark ⵜ stands for 5 animals.

② There are _____ types of animals on Uncle Tim's farm.

③ The animal greatest in number is _____ . There are _____ on the farm.

④ The animal fewest in number is _____ . There are _____ on the farm.

⑤ There are equal numbers of _____ and _____ .

⑥ There are _____ more sheep than cows.

⑦ There are _____ fewer ducks than hens.

⑧ There are altogether _____ animals on Uncle Tim's farm.

The tally chart below shows what the children have for lunch. Answer the questions and complete the bar graph.

Hot dog	Hamburger	Pizza	Fried chicken wing	Others
⊬⊬ |||	⊬⊬		||||	||||	|||

⑨ How many children choose hot dog for lunch?   _____ children

⑩ How many fewer children choose hamburger than hot dog?   _____ fewer

⑪ How many more children choose hamburger than pizza?   _____ more

⑫ Which 2 food items are chosen by the same number of children?

_____

⑬ How many children are there in Ms. Beatty's class?   _____ children

⑭ What does the word 'Others' mean in the tally chart? Suggest an example that may be included in this column.

_____

_____

⑮

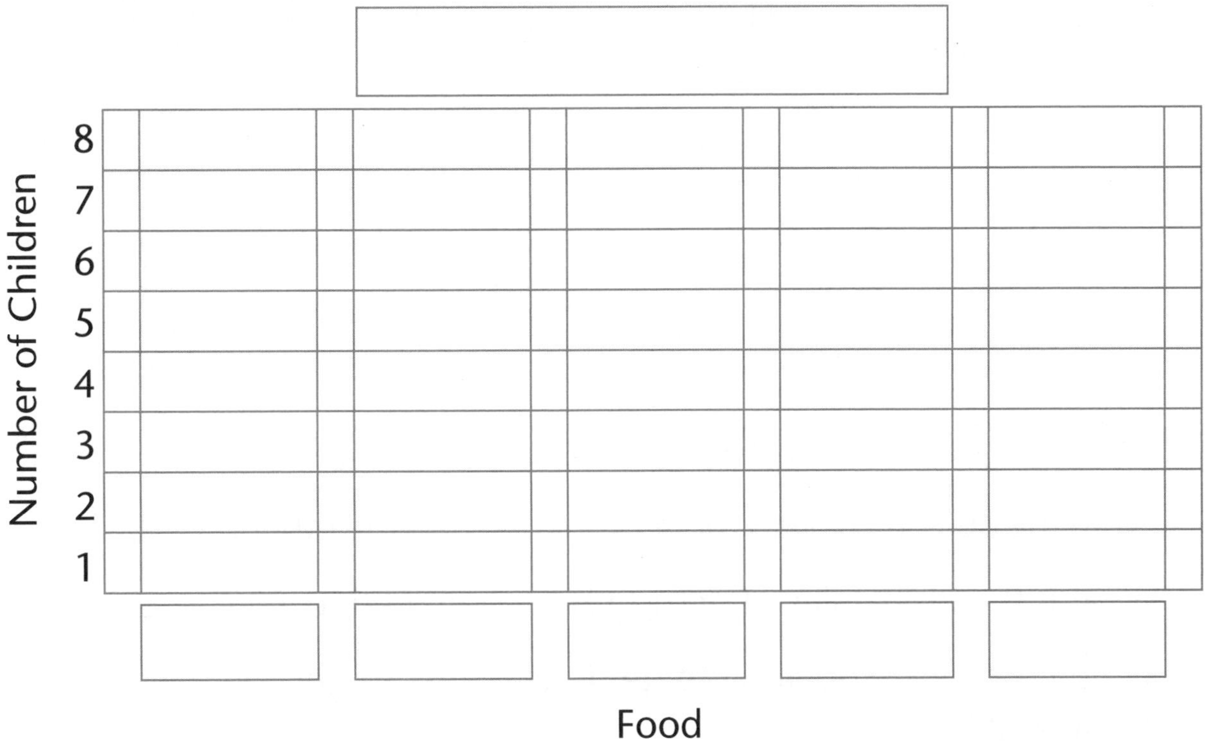

Number of Children

8
7
6
5
4
3
2
1

Food

The children use a spinner to determine what activity to go for after lunch. Look at the spinner below and compare the outcomes with the words given.

More probable	Equally probable	Less probable

⑯ Landing on A compared to B _____

⑰ Landing on C compared to A _____

⑱ Landing on B compared to C _____

⑲ Landing on B compared to A _____

⑳ Why is it more probable to land on A than B with this spinner?

_____

_____

Janice and Pete toss two coins to decide who gets an extra lollipop. Organize all the possible outcomes using a tree diagram and answer the questions.

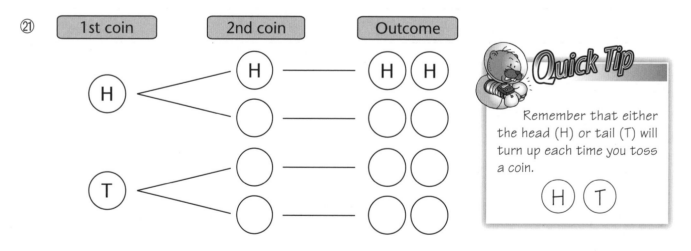

㉒ How many possible outcomes are there in all? _____

㉓ Write the outcome that is more probable than the others. _____

㉔ What is the probability of getting H H compared to T T? _____

㉕ Which outcome should Pete get if he wants to get the extra treat? _____

Uncle Tim has two prizes for the children. Each child draws a 3-D shape on a card and the one with the shape that meets the criteria set will win. Write the children's names in the boxes to find out which two can take the prizes.

㉖
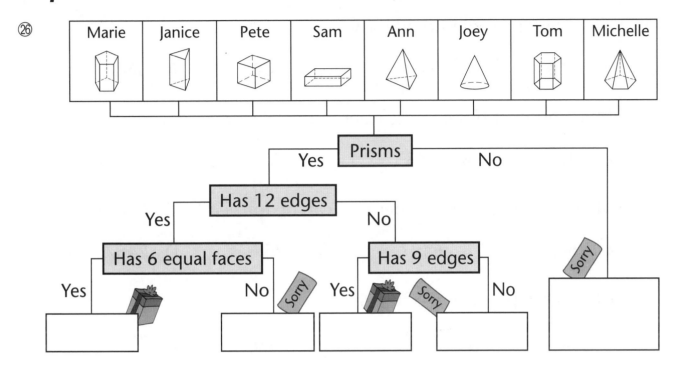

| Marie | Janice | Pete | Sam | Ann | Joey | Tom | Michelle |

㉗ Which two shapes should the children draw to get the prizes? _____

㉘ Are there any other shapes that meet the criteria for getting the prizes? _____

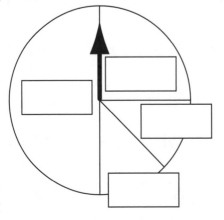

MIND BOGGLER

The children used the spinner on the right to decide the drinks they would get. Read the results and label the spinner.

➻ Janice spun 6 times and got 'Coke' 3 times.

➻ Marie spun 8 times and got 'Hot chocolate' 2 times.

➻ Michelle spun 20 times; she got 'Milk' 5 times and 'Juice' 5 times.

Circle the letter which represents the correct answer in each problem.

① Five thousand six hundred forty is _____ .

    A. 5064   B. 5046   C. 5604   D. 5640

② Which number has 4 in the hundredths place?

    A. 1403   B. 1.43   C. 1.34   D. 14.03

③ What is the greatest number that can be formed by 7, 2, 4, 6?

    A. 7642   B. 6427   C. 4267   D. 2467

④ What is the product of 530 x 4?

    A. 212   B. 2020   C. 2120   D. 202

⑤ What is the remainder of 71 ÷ 6?

    A. 5   B. 11   C. 6   D. 1

⑥ _____ ÷ 5 = 121R3

    A. 605   B. 368   C. 363   D. 608

⑦ The fraction $\frac{47}{100}$ expressed as a decimal is _____ .

    A. 4.7   B. 0.47   C. 4.07   D. 47.0

⑧ Four and nine hundredths is _____ .

    A. 4.9   B. 0.49   C. 4.09   D. 4.90

⑨ Which is a proper fraction?

    A. $\frac{3}{5}$ B. $\frac{5}{5}$ C. $\frac{6}{5}$ D. $1\frac{3}{5}$

⑩ Which of the following are parallel lines?

A.  B.   C.   D.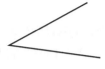

⑪ Which is the reflection image of ?

A.   B.   C.   D.

⑫ Which is the image of after a quarter-turn?

A.   B.   C. D.

⑬ The height of Janice is 105 _____ .

A. millimetres   B. centimetres   C. decimetres   D. metres

⑭ The mass of Baby Johnny is _____ .

A. 10.5 kg   B. 105 g   C. 10.5 g   D. 105 kg

⑮ The capacity of Marie's water bottle is _____ .

A. 45 mL   B. 4.5 L   C. 450 mL   D. 4.5 mL

⑯ The floor area of Pete's bedroom is _____ .

A. 64 m^2 B. 6400 cm^2 C. 6.4 m^2 D. 640 cm^2

⑰ How much change will Michelle get if she pays for a model that costs $28.76 with a $50 bill?

A. $22.34   B. $21.34   C. $31.24   D. $21.24

⑱ How many years are there in 3 centuries 5 decades?

A. 3500   B. 350   C. 305   D. 3050

Help Janice draw a similar figure and a congruent figure for the triangle. Use a protractor to measure angles A, B, and C.

⑲

B

A   C

⑳

	A	B	C
Angle			

Pete wants to make skeletons of 3-D shapes with toothpicks and plasticine. Help him draw the shapes in the boxes and fill in the numbers or names of the shapes.

㉑ a.

Triangular prism

b. It has _____ edges and _____ vertices.

c. It has _____ faces. 2 faces are _____ and _____ faces are rectangles.

㉒ a.

Rectangular pyramid

b. It has _____ edges and _____ vertices.

c. It has _____ faces. 1 face is a _____ and _____ faces are triangles.

㉓ a.

Rectangular prism

b. It has _____ edges and _____ vertices.

c. It has _____ faces. The shape of all faces is _____ .

68

Look at the shapes on the centimetre grid paper. Answer the questions and draw the diagrams.

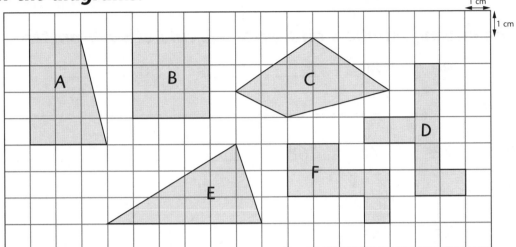

㉔ Which shapes are quadrilaterals? _____

㉕ What is the area of each shape?

㉖ What is the perimeter of each of the following shapes?

㉗ Draw a rectangle G which has the same area as B but a different perimeter. Label the perimeter of G.

㉘ Draw a rectangle H which has the same perimeter as B but a different area. Label the area of H.

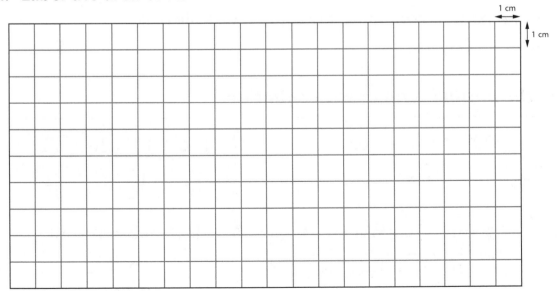

Final Test

Fill in the missing numbers and write the rule of each pattern.

㉙ 100   90   80   _____   _____   50   _____   _____

Rule _____

㉚ 80   78   74   68   _____   _____   _____   _____

Rule _____

㉛ 60   58   61   59   62   _____   _____   _____

Rule _____

㉜ 25   26   28   31   _____   _____   _____   _____

Rule _____

Look at Michelle's saving pattern. Complete the table and answer the question.

Day 1   Day 2   Day 3

㉝

Day	1	2	3	4	5	6	7
Number of coins							

㉞ If the pattern continues, how much will Michelle save on Day 10? $ _____

Find the missing term in each equation.

㉟ $200 - 100 = a + 65$

a = _____

㊱ $b - 48 = 38 + 62$

b = _____

㊲ $56 + m = 10 \times 8$

m = _____

㊳ $163 - 43 = n - 50$

n = _____

Pete is designing a symmetrical shape. Help him complete the shape on the grid below.

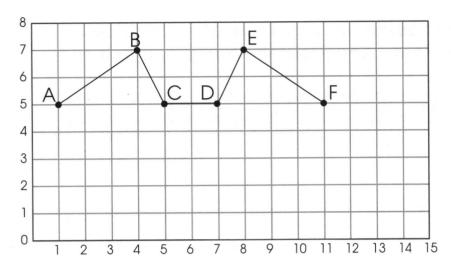

㊴ Write the coordinates of the following points.

A (_____ , _____)   B (_____ , _____)   C (_____ , _____)

D (_____ , _____)   E (_____ , _____)   F (_____ , _____)

㊵ Locate the following points on the grid.

G (13 , 5)   H (13 , 3)   I (11 , 3)   J (8 , 1)

K (7 , 3)   L (5 , 3)   M (4 , 1)   N(1 , 3)

㊶ Complete the shape by joining the points in alphabetical order from A to N, and then from N to A.

㊷ Draw and label the line of symmetry of the shape completed in ㊶.

㊸ Which are their possible translation images? Give one example each.

a. line BC _____   b. line CD _____

㊹ Which are their reflection images about the line of symmetry?

a. line ABC _____   b. line DEF _____

㊺ Which are their possible rotation images? Give one example each.

a. line CD _____   b. line AB _____

㊻ Pete wants to change the shape so that it will have 1 more line of symmetry. Help him shade the part that should be cut out from the shape in ㊶. Draw and label the new line of symmetry of the shape.

Final Test

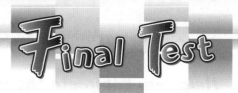

The tally chart below shows the number of coloured marbles Janice has. Complete the bar graph and the sentences.

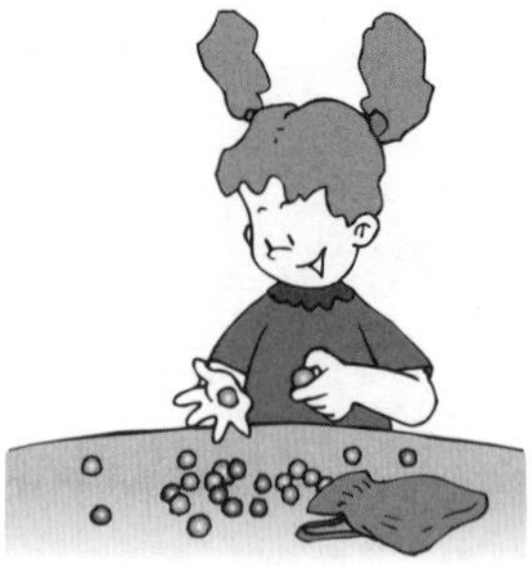

㊼

Red	Green	Yellow	Blue	White
𝍸	𝍸 𝍸 ||	||	𝍸	𝍸 |

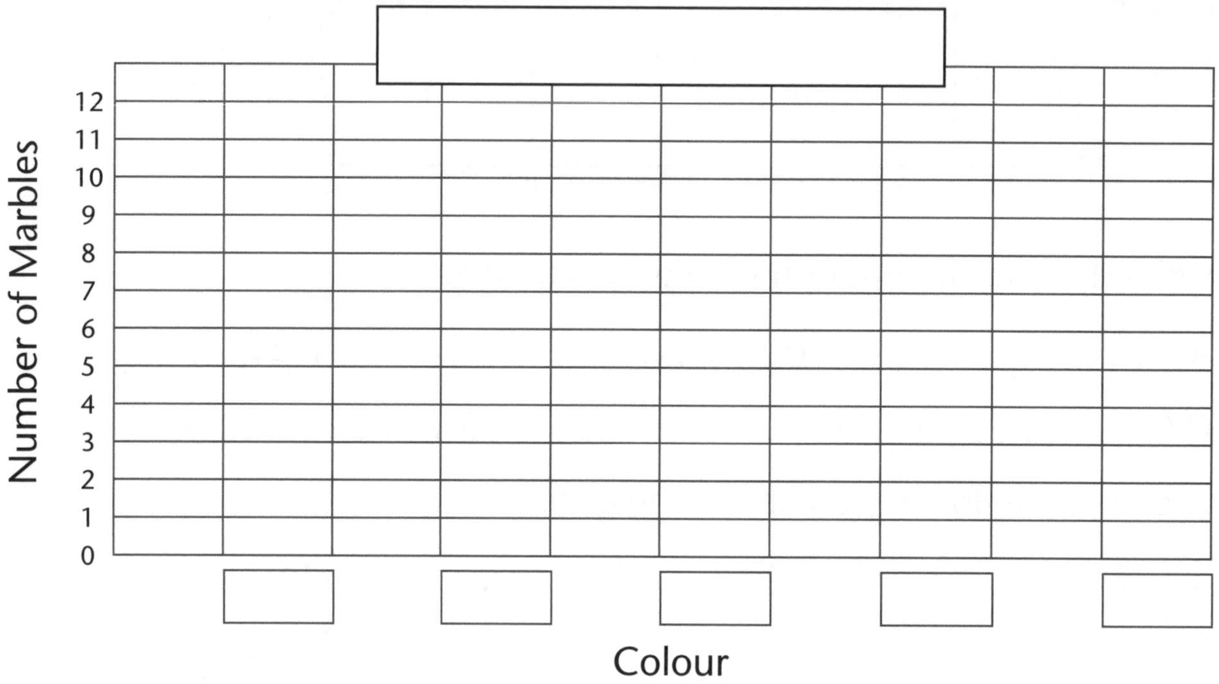

12
11
10
9
8
7
6
5
4
3
2
1
0
Number of Marbles
Colour

㊽ The marbles greatest in number are ________ .

㊾ The marbles fewest in number are ________ .

㊿ There are ________ more green marbles than yellow marbles.

(51) There are the same number of ________ marbles and ________ marbles.

(52) Janice has ________ marbles in all.

(53) ________ of Janice's marbles are not white.

(54) Compare the probability of picking a marble from Janice's collection using 'More probable', 'Equally probable', or 'Less probable'.

a. a red marble vs to a blue one ________________

b. a green marble vs to a white one ________________

c. a yellow marble vs to a green one ________________

Review

1. 973	2. 297	3. 489
4. 859	5. 338	6. 792
7. 773	8. 56	9. 177
10. 437	11. 14	12. 7
13. 7	14. 14	15. 38
16. 12	17. 72	18. 42
19. 20	20. 27	

21.
$$\begin{array}{r} 4 \\ 3\overline{\smash)12} \\ \underline{12} \end{array}$$
22.
$$\begin{array}{r} 3 \\ 9\overline{\smash)27} \\ \underline{27} \end{array}$$
23.
$$\begin{array}{r} 5 \\ 7\overline{\smash)35} \\ \underline{35} \end{array}$$

24.
$$\begin{array}{r} 8 \\ 6\overline{\smash)48} \\ \underline{48} \end{array}$$
25.
$$\begin{array}{r} 3\,R\,2 \\ 8\overline{\smash)26} \\ \underline{24} \\ 2 \end{array}$$
26.
$$\begin{array}{r} 9\,R\,2 \\ 5\overline{\smash)47} \\ \underline{45} \\ 2 \end{array}$$

27.
$$\begin{array}{r} 5\,R\,1 \\ 9\overline{\smash)46} \\ \underline{45} \\ 1 \end{array}$$
28.
$$\begin{array}{r} 8\,R\,2 \\ 4\overline{\smash)34} \\ \underline{32} \\ 2 \end{array}$$

29. 16	30. 35	31. 12
32. 5	33. 7R3	34. 6R2
35. cm	36. m	37. km
38. m	39. km	

40. A. g   B. kg   C. kg   D. g   E. kg

41. A, D, C, E, B	42. 11:45	43. 5:10
44. 8:20	45. 4	46. 2
47. 1	48. $\frac{1}{4}$	49. $\frac{2}{3}$
50. $\frac{3}{5}$	51. $\frac{1}{2}$	52. $\frac{2}{5}$
53. $\frac{1}{3}$	54. 10 ; 11 ; 12	
55. C, B, A	56. Rotation	57. Translation
58. Reflection	59. 13 ; 21	60. △ ; ○

61. Rectangular prism ; 6 ; 12 ; 8
62. Triangular pyramid or Tetrahedron ; 4 ; 6 ; 4
63. Square pyramid or Pyramid ; 5 ; 8 ; 5
64. Triangular prism ; 5 ; 9 ; 6

65. Hamburger	66. 8	67. Taco
68. 2.24	69. 0.75	70. 6

1   Numbers to 10 000

1. 2347	2. 3158	3. 4409

4. Five thousand two hundred thirty-nine
5. Seven thousand one hundred eight
6. Four thousand six hundred twenty
7. Three thousand fifty-seven

8. 6453	9. 9081	10. 8506
11. 5740	12. 5704	13. 1829
14. 3065	15. 9420	16. 2 ; 6 ; 8 ; 0
17. 7 ; 9 ; 6 ; 3	18. 4 ; 2 ; 2 ; 6	19. 500 ; 80 ; 6
20. 2000 ; 50 ; 5	21. 8000 ; 400 ; 3	22. 3267
23. 6038	24. 5740	25. hundreds

26. tens	27. thousands	28. ones
29. a. 8974 b. 2310		30. a. 3653 b. 1930
31. 5993 ; 5693 ; 5593		32. 4102 ; 5102 ; 7102
33. 5364 ; 5464 ; 5774		34. 3210
35. 3457	36. 1683	37. 9542
38. Tom	39. Marie	40. 9536
41. 6436	42. 6843	43. 7463
44. 7463 ; 6436		45. 7463 ; 7536
46. 9536 ; 7536		47. 7536 ; 6436

48. 6436 ; 6843 ; 7463 ; 7536 ; 9536

Mind Boggler

GREAT WORK

2   Addition and Subtraction

1. 8039	2. 9812	3. 3637
4. 4669	5. 6547	6. 5526
7. 6558	8. 6003	9. 10 330
10. 7205	11. 7173	12. 3911
13. 7461	14. 9822	15. 4702
16. 9011	17. 7618	18. 11 715
19. 8495	20. 8824	21. 8129
22. 3934	23. 6053	24. 6659

25.

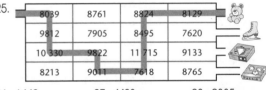

26. 6442	27. 4423	28. 9335
29. 5477	30. 2297	31. 7115
32. 3641	33. 4828	34. 5529
35. 1749	36. 3724	37. 3725
38. 3270	39. 8401	40. 5380
41. 300	42. 300	43. 500
44. 200	45. 500	46. 100
47. 7000	48. 5000	49. 2000
50. 7000	51. 5000	52. 8000

53. 10 000 ; 7000 ; 3000 ; 10 000
54. 8990 ; 6000 ; 3000 ; 9000
55. 5935 ; 7000 ; 600 ; 6400
56. 3186 ; 2000 ; 1000 ; 3000
57. 8533 ; 9000 ; 700 ; 8300
58. 8861 ; 5000 ; 4000 ; 9000
59. 7271 ; 8000 ; 400 ; 7600
60. 6596 ; 5000 ; 2000 ; 7000
61. 780 ; 1000 ; 300 ; 700

62. 5003	63. 6524	64. $1200
65. 8	66. 2	67. 2
68. 1999		

69. a. 1125 + 2540 ; 3665 ; 3665   b. 2540 − 970 ; 1570 ; 1570
70. a. 3411 + 2936 ; 6347 ; 6347   b. 3411 − 424 ; 2987 ; 2987

A n s w e r s

Mind Boggler

9367 ; 584

3 Multiplication

1. 700
2. 90
3. 8000
4. 50
5. 2000
6. 600
7. 3000
8. 1200
9. 15 000
10. 240
11. 200
12. 2400
13. 6000
14. 1200
15. 8000
16. 2800
17. 10 000
18. 180
19. 2000
20. 560
21. 450
22. 360
23. 6300
24. 1600
25. 8000
26. 3000
27. 280
28. 27 000
29. 3600

30.
```
    16
x    7
    42
    70
   112
```

31.
```
    43
x    5
    15
   200
   215
```
32.
```
    25
x    8
    40
   160
   200
```
33.
```
    52
x    4
     8
   200
   208
```

34. 432
35. 470
36. 196
37. 456
38. 138
39. 152
40. 612
41. 644
42. 252
43. 324
44. 608
45. 215
46. 318
47. 567
48. 75
49. 272
50. 310
51. 102
52. 216
53. 424
54. 306
55. 322

56.
```
   436
x    7
    42
   210
  2800
  3052
```
57.
```
   352
x    8
    16
   400
  2400
  2816
```

58. 2072
59. 2390
60. 5751
61. 2292
62. 1694
63. 2916
64. 3168
65. 2104
66. 5550
67. 5184
68. 2716
69. 1018
70. 915
71. 2125
72. 5724
73. 3560
74. 432
75. 2700
76. 1589

77. 275 x 7 = 1925 ; They picked 1925 apples.

78. 55 x 6 = 330

    330 students have been on the bus in just one day.

79. 125 x 5 = 625 ; 625 people can sit in the bleachers.

80. 24 x 7 = 168 ; Amanda will have to sell 168 packages of cookies.

Mind Boggler

32

4 Division I

1. 8 ; 4 ; 40
2. 9 ; 3 ; 300
3. 16 ; 4 ; 40
4. 45 ; 9 ; 90
5. 36 ; 6 ; 60
6. 7 ; 1 ; 100

7. 80
8. 30
9. 10
10. 20
11. 70
12. 100
13. 90
14. 70
15. 30
16. 20
17. 30
18. 50
19. 60 ; 20
20. 80 ; 20
21. 50 ; 10
22. 300 ; 50
23. 80 ; 40
24. 800 ; 100
25. 350 ; 50
26. 540 ; 60

27.
```
    18
2 | 36
    2
    16
    16
```
28.
```
    16
3 | 48
    3
    18
    18
```

29.
```
    15
5 | 75
    5
    25
    25
```
30.
```
    15
6 | 90
    6
    30
    30
```

31. 13
32. 12
33. 11
34. 37
35. 18
36. 14
37. 18
38. 25
39. 14
40. 13
41. 90 ÷ 9 ; 10
42. 81 ÷ 3 ; 27
43. 68 ÷ 4 ; 17

44.
```
    24 R 1
3 | 73
    6
    13
    12
     1
```
45.
```
    16 R 4
5 | 84
    5
    34
    30
     4
```
46.
```
    15 R 2
6 | 92
    6
    32
    30
     2
```

47.
```
    34 R 1
2 | 69
    6
     9
     8
     1
```
48.
```
    13 R 1
4 | 53
    4
    13
    12
     1
```
49.
```
    11 R 2
8 | 90
    8
    10
     8
     2
```

50.
```
    12 R 5
7 | 89
    7
    19
    14
     5
```
51.
```
    10 R 2
9 | 92
    9
     2
     0
     2
```
52.
```
    13 R 3
6 | 81
    6
    21
    18
     3
```

53.
```
    47 R 1
2 | 95
    8
    15
    14
     1
```
54.
```
    19 R 2
5 | 97
    5
    47
    45
     2
```

55. 16 ; 1
56. 13 ; 2
57. 18 ; 1
58. 12 ; 3
59. 16 ; 2
60. 12 ; 2
61. oranges
62. 5 ; 14 ; 70
63. 4 ; 21 ; 84
64. 3 ; 23 ; 69
65. 6 ; 16 ; 96

66. The product of the divisor and the quotient is equal to the dividend.

67. 96 ÷ 4 ; 24 ; 24

68. 92 ÷ 6 ; 15 R 2 ; 15 ; 2

Mind Boggler

4

74

5 Division II

1.
```
    211
  4)844
    8
    4
    4
     4
     4
```

2.
```
    245
  3)735
    6
    13
    12
     15
     15
```

3.
```
    136
  5)680
    5
    18
    15
     30
     30
```

4. 282
5. 144
6. 116
7. 119
8. 112
9. 213
10. 325
11. 128
12. 113
13. 214

14.
```
    31
  6)186
    18
     6
     6
```

15.
```
    42
  9)378
    36
    18
    18
```

16.
```
    65
  7)455
    42
    35
    35
```

17. 51
18. 32
19. 76
20. 84
21. 37
22. 93
23. 45
24. 66
25. 22
26. 48
27. 56
28. 39
29. 25
30. 74

31.
963 ÷ 9		204		856 ÷ 8
612 ÷ 3		107		610 ÷ 2
545 ÷ 5		305		816 ÷ 4
616 ÷ 2		308		654 ÷ 6
915 ÷ 3		109		924 ÷ 3

32. 104 ; 5 ; 270
33. ✔ ; 305 ; 3 ; 915
34. ✔ ; 102 ; 6 ; 612
35. 99 ; 94 ; 8 ; 752
36. ✔ ; 99 ; 9 ; 891
37. 243 ; 248 ; 4 ; 992

38.
```
     90 R 1
  7)631
    63
     1
```

39.
```
    100 R 4
  8)804
    8
    4
```

40.
```
    194 R 3
  4)779
    4
    37
    36
    19
    16
     3
```

41.
```
     45 R 2
  6)272
    24
    32
    30
     2
```

42. 80 R 1
43. 40 R 1
44. 24 R 4
45. 68 R 4
46. 47 R 2
47. 157 R 1
48. 224 R 2
49. 370 R 1
50. 4 ; 101 ; 1 ; 405
51. 7 ; 56 ; 5 ; 397
52. 5 ; 144 ; 1 ; 721
53. 8 ; 80 ; 3 ; 643
54. The sum is equal to the dividend.
55. 114 ; 0 ; ✔
56. 88 ; ✔
57. 121 ; 2
58. 97 ; 5
59. 76 ; 0 ; ✔
60. 104 ; 0 ; ✔
61. 85 ; 4
62. 66 ; 4
63. 91 ; 0 ; ✔
64. 6 ; 7 ; 8

Mind Boggler
57

6 Fractions

1. $\frac{3}{4}$
2. $\frac{1}{4}$
3. $\frac{1}{4}$
4. $\frac{1}{4}$
5. $\frac{9}{15}$
6. $\frac{6}{15}$
7. a. $\frac{1}{8}$ b. $\frac{4}{8}$ c. $\frac{3}{8}$
8. green : $\frac{7}{9}$, $\frac{8}{15}$, $\frac{1}{5}$
   yellow : $\frac{8}{8}$, $\frac{11}{10}$, $\frac{10}{6}$
   red : $1\frac{3}{4}$, $2\frac{1}{3}$, $3\frac{1}{2}$
9. $3\frac{2}{6}$
10. $2\frac{5}{12}$
11. $\frac{10}{8}$
12. $\frac{5}{4}$
13. $\frac{15}{10}$

14. a.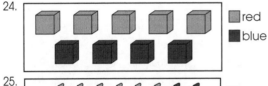
b. $\frac{1}{5}$, $\frac{3}{5}$, $\frac{4}{5}$

15. a.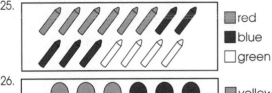
b. $\frac{2}{8}$, $\frac{5}{8}$, $\frac{7}{8}$

16. >
17. <
18. <
19. >
20. >
21. >
22. $\frac{13}{12}$, $\frac{11}{12}$, $\frac{7}{12}$
23. $3\frac{4}{5}$, $3\frac{1}{5}$, $2\frac{1}{5}$

24.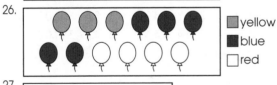
□ red
■ blue

25.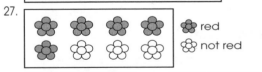
□ red
■ blue
□ green

26.
□ yellow
■ blue
□ red

27.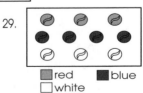
🌸 red
🌼 not red

28.
[faces image]
2

29.
[beans image]
■ red ■ blue
□ white
3

30. $\frac{2}{10}$; 0.2
31. $\frac{4}{10}$; 0.4
32. $\frac{9}{100}$; 0.09
33. $\frac{18}{100}$; 0.18
34. $\frac{59}{100}$; 0.59

35.
[grid] 0.7

36.
[grid] 0.05

37.
[grid] 0.42

Mind Boggler

🍎🍎🍎🍎🍎🍎🍎🍎🍎🍎🍐🍐 ; $\frac{2}{12}$

7   Decimals

1. Two tenths
2. Five hundredths
3. Seventy-four hundredths
4. Ninety-one hundredths
5. 0.4
6. 0.08
7. 0.12
8. 0.67

9.		5	2	
10.		7	4	9
11.	5	8	1	

12. hundredths ; 0.06
13. tenths ; 0.4
14. ones ; 7
15. hundredths ; 0.09
16. >
17. <
18. <
19. <
20. 0.07, 0.1, 1.4
21. 2.02, 2.20, 20.2
22. 3.04, 3.42, 4.32
23. 4
24. 1
25. 3
26 1
27. 3
28. 4
29. 0.4 ; 0.5 ; 0.9
30. 0.2 ; 0.4 ; 0.6
31. 0.7 ; 0.5 ; 0.2
32. 0.6 ; 0.3 ; 0.3
33. 1.5 ; 1.3 ; 2.8
34. 2.3
35. 3.8
36. 26.3
37. 64.9
38. 19.0
39. 16.8
40. 50.6
41. 26.4
42. 88.7
43. 41.1
44. 86.4
45. 126.2
46. 6.2
47. 6.4
48. 2.8
49. 2.9
50. 7.5
51. 9.9
52. 25.3
53. 47.6
54. 60.9
55. 90.5
56. 52.7
57. 61.4
58. 39.2 ;
$$\begin{array}{r} 1\,2 \\ +\,2\,7 \\ \hline 3\,9 \end{array}$$
59. 24.9 ;
$$\begin{array}{r} 4\,3 \\ -\,1\,8 \\ \hline 2\,5 \end{array}$$
60. 2.1 + 1.7 ; 3.8 ; 3.8
61. 3.8 – 3.3 ; 0.5 ; 0.5
62. 1.1 + 3.3 ; 4.4 ; 4.4
63. 4.4 – 3.9 ; 0.5 ; 0.5

Mind Boggler

Danny ; Tom ; Pete ; 6.1

Progress Test

1. hundredths ; thousands ; tens ; tenths ; hundreds
2. 0.03 ; 4000 ; 20 ; 0.1 ; 500
3. 6350
4. 7829
5. 0.42
6. 2003
7. 36.09
8. Twenty-five and thirteen hundredths
9. Seven hundredths
10. Nine tenths
11. Four thousand twenty-eight
12. Seven thousand five hundred six
13. 700 ; 90 ; 3
14. 3 ; 0 ; 7 ; 5
15. 5089
16. 4605
17. 30.19
18. 5193 ; 5293 ; 5493
19. 8080 ; 6080 ; 5080
20. 0.39 ; 0.49 ; 0.69
21. 1.33 ; 1.3 ; 1.03
22. 5.64 ; 5.46 ; 5.06
23. 8736 ; 8973 ; 9736
24. $\frac{3}{15}$; $\frac{9}{15}$; $\frac{11}{15}$; $\frac{17}{15}$

25. $2\frac{7}{9}$; $2\frac{3}{9}$; $1\frac{3}{9}$; $1\frac{1}{9}$
26. $\frac{7}{10}$; 0.7
27. 0.79
28. $\frac{6}{100}$
29. I
30. M
31. P
32. I
33. M
34. I
35. P
36. P
37. 5525
38. 324
39. 7544
40. 7359
41.
$$\begin{array}{r} 60\text{ R}3 \\ 4\overline{)243} \\ \underline{24} \\ 3 \end{array}$$
42.
$$\begin{array}{r} 17\text{ R}1 \\ 5\overline{)86} \\ \underline{5} \\ 36 \\ \underline{35} \\ 1 \end{array}$$
43.
$$\begin{array}{r} 126 \\ 6\overline{)756} \\ \underline{6} \\ 15 \\ \underline{12} \\ 36 \\ \underline{36} \end{array}$$
44.
$$\begin{array}{r} 35\text{ R}3 \\ 7\overline{)248} \\ \underline{21} \\ 38 \\ \underline{35} \\ 3 \end{array}$$
45. 25.4
46. 55.9
47. 44.2
48. 3.6
49. 55.1
50. 13.3
51. 432
52. 5635
53. 12
54. 108
55. 3252
56. 6329
57. ♥ red ♥ yellow ♥ blue   a. 5   b. yellow   c. Red
58. 3468 ÷ 6 ; 578 ; 578
59. 3468 + 1020 ; 4488 ; 4488
60. 4488 – 615 ; 3873 ; 3873
61. 837 x 4 ; 3348 ; 3348
62. 1.2 + 0.4 ; 1.6 ; 1.6
63. 1.6 + 0.5 – 0.2 ; 1.9 ; 1.9

8   Geometry I

1. A
2. C
3. B
4. C
5. A
6. C
7. B
8. 30°
9. 45°
10. 60°
11. 90°
12. 135°
13. 120°
14. 75°
15.
16. Trapezoid ; Square ; Rhombus ; Rectangle ; Parallelogram
17. B ; C
18. D ; E
19. B ; C ; D ; E
20. A
21. B ; D
22. Rectangle
23. Rhombus
24. Trapezoid

25. Parallelogram   26. Square
27. Cylinder

28. Rectangular pyramid
29. Rectangular prism

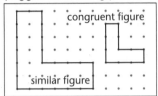

30. 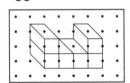   12 ; 8

31. 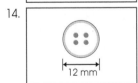   10 ; 6

32. A and G, D and L, E and H, C and K
33. A and M, G and M, B and D, B and L, F and I
34. (Suggested drawings)

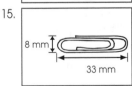

Mind Boggler

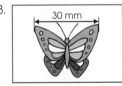

9   Units of Measure

1. cm   2. km   3. m
4. m   5. mm   6. cm
7. mm   8. 105 ; 10.5
9. 82 ; 8.2   10. 95 ; 9.5   11. 68 ; 6.8
12. 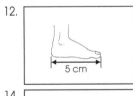   13.

14.   15.

16. 2   17. 5   18. 3
19. 80   20. 50   21. 250
22. 1 ; 3 ; 4 23. 25 ; 33 ; 31 ; 20 ; 32 ; 30
24. Joey   25. Pete   26. 5
27. Marie   28. Sam   29. Pete ; Sam
30. $29.56   31. $20.42   32. $28.77
33. $29.63   34. $10.13   35. $1.05

36. Sam   37. Tom   38. $75.65
39. $51.67
40. Change : $35 – $26.37 = $8.63 ; photo frame
41. Total price : $14.63 + $35.49 = $50.12 ; does not have
42. Total price : $35.49 + $8.51 = $44.00 ; 4
43. Total price : $14.63 + $8.51 + $26.37 = $49.51
    a clock, a photo frame and a snow globe

Mind Boggler

a table lamp, a photo frame and a snow globe

10   Perimeter and Area

1. area ; m^2 2. perimeter ; cm
3. perimeter ; m   4. area ; m^2
5. area ; cm^2 6. 12
7. 13   8. 8   9. B   10. C
11. 19 cm ; 24 cm ; 26 cm ; 62 cm ; 30cm ; 36 cm
12. 14 cm ; 12 cm ; 12 cm ; 12 cm
13. 8 cm^2 ; 5 cm^2 ; 9 cm^2 ; 7 cm^2
14. P   15. R
16. No   17. 7 cm^2
18. 9 cm^2 19. 9 cm^2
20. 12 cm^2
21.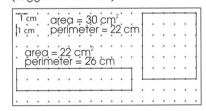

22. different
23. (Suggested answers)

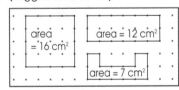

24. different

Mind Boggler

(Suggested answers)

11   Capacity, Volume and Mass

1. litre   2. litre   3. millilitre
4. millilitre   5. millilitre   6. millilitre
7. litre   8. litre   9. litre
10. millilitre 11. litre   12. 4

77

13. 2   14. 3   15. 3

16. 6   17. 4

18. mug , syrup , detergent , milk carton , bucket

19. $4 \, cm^3$ 20. $6 \, cm^3$ 21. $12 \, cm^3$

22. $8 \, cm^3$ 23. $9 \, cm^3$ 24. $7 \, cm^3$

25. $5 \, cm^3$

26. a. (Suggested answers)

 b. Yes c. No d. No

27. kilogram   28. gram

29. gram   30. milligram

31. gram   32. kilogram

33. gram   34. milligram

35. 200 g   36. Cornflakes

37. Sausages   38. Black pepper

39. Cornflakes   40. 250 g

41. 10 kg , 950 g , 750 g , 550 g , 55 g

42. A   43. B   44. C

45. 3.5 kg 46. 900 g 47. 2100 g

48. g   49. mg 50. g

51. kg

Mind Boggler

 1. 4 pigs   2. 1 calf , 1 pig and 1 tiger

12 Geometry II

 1. Reflection 2. Translation 3. Rotation

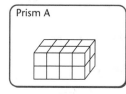 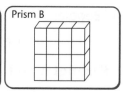

6.

 7. A ; C   8. A ; B ; D 9. C ; D

10.-11. (Suggested drawings)

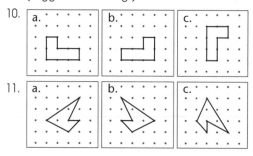

12. 2 ; up ; 5 ; right

13. 3 ; down ; 8 ; right

14. 2 ; up ; 3 ; left

15. 1 ; down ; 10 ; left

16. a. quarter b. full c. half

17.

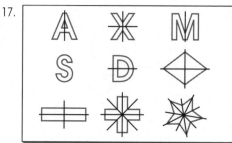

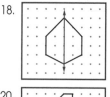 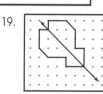

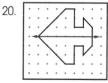 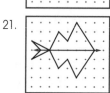

22. a. (1 , 6) b. (9 , 9) c. (4 , 1)

  d. (10 , 8) e. (10 , 10) f. (9 , 2)

23. a. Pool b. Pond c. Water slide

  d. Store e. Basketball court f. Sand box

Mind Boggler

 Pond ; Picnic area ; Pool

13 Patterns and Simple Equations

 1. 24 ; 27 ; 30 ; 33 ; 36 2. 60 ; 64 ; 68 ; 72 ; 76

 3. 55 ; 50 ; 40 ; 35 ; 30 4. 42 ; 36 ; 24 ; 18 ; 12

 5. 35 ; 42 ; 56 ; 63 ; 70 6. 32 ; 40 ; 48 ; 64 ; 72

 7. 54 ; 45 ; 36 ; 27 ; 18 8. 40 ; 50 ; 70 ; 90 ; 100

 9.   10. ☐ ○

 11. ☐ ◭   12. ⊕ ⊕

13. 11   14. 36

15. 69 ; 73 ; 77 ; Add 4. 16. 51 ; 44 ; 37 ; Subtract 7.

17. 63 ; 55 ; 61 ; Add 6, subtract 8.

18. 81 ; 75 ; 68 ; Subtract 1, subtract 2, subtract 3...

19. 64 ; 128 ; 256 ; Double each number.

20. 48 ; 66 ; 87 ; Go up by the 3 times table.

21. a. 7 , 10 , 13 , 16 , 19 ; 3 , 6 , 9 , 12 , 15 b. 19 ; 15

22. 12 ; 14 ; 16 ; 18 23. 12 ; 16 ; 20 ; 24

24. 6 ; 8 ; 10 ; 12 25. 5 ; 6 ; 7 ; 8

26. 1 ; 4 ; 9 ; 16 ; 25 ; 36 27. 12 ; 12

28. 9 ; 4 , 9   29. 16 ; 2 , 16

30. 19 ; 23 , 19   31. 3

32. 5   33. 6   34. 1

35. 23   36. 16   37. 35

38. 3

Mind Boggler

 1. 20 ; 10 ; 4   2. 4 ; 2 ; 1 ; 2 ; 1

14 Graphs and Probability

1.
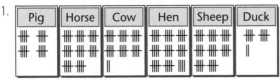

Pig	Horse	Cow	Hen	Sheep	Duck

2. six
3. hen ; 42 hens
4. duck ; 12 ducks
5. horses ; sheep
6. 8
7. 32
8. 188
9. 8
10. 2
11. 2
12. Pizza and fried chicken wing
13. 25
14. 'Others' column includes foods that are not on the list of the tally, e.g. sandwiches.

15.
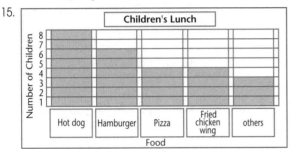

16. More probable
17. Less probable
18. Equally probable
19. Less probable
20. (Suggested answer)

It is more probable to stop on A because sector A is greater than sector B.

21.
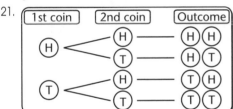

22. 4
23. TH or HT
24. Equally probable
25. TH or HT
26. Pete ; Sam ; Janice ; Marie, Tom ; Ann, Joey, Michelle
27. Cube and triangular prism
28. No

Mind Boggler

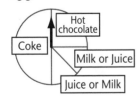

Final Test

1. D	2. C	3. A
4. C	5. A	6. D
7. B	8. C	9. A
10. B	11. D	12. C
13. B	14. A	15. C

16. A
17. D
18. B
19. (Suggested drawings)

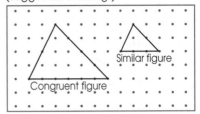

20. 63° ; 72° ; 45°

21. a.
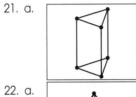
b. 9 ; 6
c. 5 ; triangles ; 3

22. a.

b. 8 ; 5
c. 5 ; rectangles ; 4

23. a.
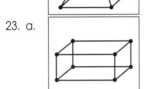
b. 12 ; 8
c. 6 ; rectangles

24. A, B, C
25. 10 cm² ; 9 cm² ; 9 cm² ; 8 cm² ; 9 cm² ; 7 cm²
26. 12 cm ; 18 cm ; 14 cm
27.-28. (Suggested answers)

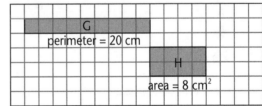

29. 70 ; 60 ; 40 ; 30 ; Subtract 10.
30. 60 ; 50 ; 38 ; 24 ; Go down by the 2 times table.
31. 60 ; 63 ; 61 ; Subtract 2, add 3.
32. 35 ; 40 ; 46 ; 53 ; Add 1, add 2, add 3...
33. 1 ; 3 ; 6 ; 10 ; 15 ; 21 ; 28
34. 13.75
35. 35
36. 148
37. 24
38. 170
39. (1 , 5) ; (4 , 7) ; (5 , 5) ; (7 , 5) ; (8 , 7) ; (11 , 5)
40.-42.

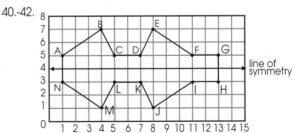

43. (Suggested answers) a. KJ b. FG
44. a. NML b. KJI
45. (Suggested answers) a. GH b. NM

46.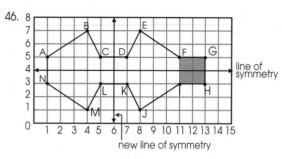

new line of symmetry

47.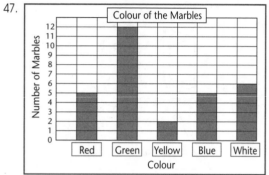

D.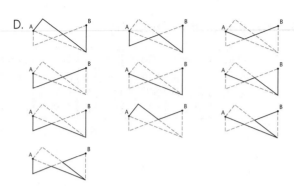

There are 10 different paths.

E.

48. green   49. yellow   50. 10

51. red ; blue   52. 30   53. 24

54. a. Equally probable   b. More probable

c. Less probable

F. Greatest difference:
```
    9 8 7 6
  -   3 4 5
  ─────────
    9 5 3 1
```

Least difference:
```
    3 4 5 6
  -   9 8 7
  ─────────
    2 4 6 9
```

Game Cards

A.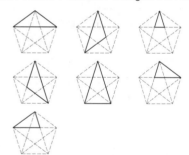

B. For each vertex, 7 different triangles can be found.

A pentagon has 5 vertices. Totally 35 triangles are found.

C. Greatest number of trials for the 1st box = 4

Greatest number of trials for the 2nd box = 3

Greatest number of trials for the 3rd box = 2

Greatest number of trials for the 4th box = 1

Greatest number of trials needed to open all 4 boxes

= 4 + 3 + 2 + 1

= 10